OXFORD

Series Editors: David Miller and

THE POLITICS OF PRESENCE

OXFORD POLITICAL THEORY

Oxford Political Theory presents the best new work in contemporary political theory. It is intended to be broad in scope, including original contributions to political philosophy, and also work in applied political theory. The series will contain works of outstanding quality with no restriction as to approach or subject matter.

THE POLITICS OF PRESENCE

ANNE PHILLIPS

CLARENDON PRESS · OXFORD

OXFORD
UNIVERSITY PRESS

Great Clarendon Street, Oxford OX2 6DP

Oxford University Press is a department of the University of Oxford.
It furthers the University's objective of excellence in research, scholarship,
and education by publishing worldwide in

Oxford New York

Auckland Bangkok Buenos Aires Cape Town Chennai
Dar es Salaam Delhi Hong Kong Istanbul Karachi Kolkata
Kuala Lumpur Madrid Melbourne Mexico City Mumbai Nairobi
São Paulo Shanghai Taipei Tokyo Toronto

Oxford is a registered trade mark of Oxford University Press
in the UK and in certain other countries

Published in the United States
by Oxford University Press Inc., New York

Printed in Great Britain by

Antony Rowe Ltd., Eastbourne

PREFACE

I began the work for this book courtesy of a Social Science Research Fellowship from the Nuffield Foundation in 1992–3, and did much of the initial writing up during a Research Fellowship at the Humanities Research Centre of the Australian National University in the first months of 1994. I am very grateful for the opportunity these two fellowships gave me. The luxury of a full year to work exclusively on one project made it possible for me to explore avenues I might otherwise have ignored; while the ANU provided just the combination of scholarly peace and intellectual stimulation that I needed to get going on writing. I am also very grateful to London Guildhall University for generously enabling me to take up the second fellowship so soon after the first.

I was able to try out some of the initial ideas at a workshop on 'Citizenship and Plurality', which took place at the Joint Sessions of the European Consortium for Political Research at the University of Leiden in April 1993; and at the Annual Conference for the Study of Political Thought (on the theme of 'Democracy and Difference'), which was held at Yale in the same month. I learnt a great deal from the participants at both, as well as from the many people who commented on later versions at universities across the UK, Ireland, and Australia. Throughout the period of writing, I benefited from numerous discussions with Wendy Stokes on issues of democracy and representation. I also benefited from various arguments with Ciaran Driver, whose sceptical response to my initial formulations helped me to clarify their basis.

Will Kymlicka, David Miller, and Iris Young made extremely helpful comments on the first draft of the book; in each case, these highlighted inadequacies I had been trying to forget, and spurred me on to address them more fully. Iwan Morgan corrected some of my misapprehensions about American politics, and Will Kymlicka corrected many of my misapprehensions about Canadian politics; neither, of course, should be held accountable for any mistakes that may have crept subsequently into the final version. Tim Barton and Dominic Byatt encouraged me through the various stages of writing, and arranged a speed of production I had thought impossible for Oxford University Press. Alok Chander and Graham Clarke calmed my fears when I thought a virus was about to wipe my disks, and helped restore my faith in computers.

My thanks to all of these for the different ways in which they made the book possible. My most heartfelt thanks, though, go to my sons Declan and Anthony, for giving me such good reasons for not working at weekends.

A.P.

ACKNOWLEDGEMENTS

Parts of Chapter 1 have already been published as 'Dealing With Difference: From a Politics of Ideas to a Politics of Presence?' in *Constellations*, 1/1 (1994): 74–91. Parts of Chapters 2 and 3 have been published as 'Democracy and Representation; or, Why should it matter who our representatives are?' in *Frauen und Politik: Schweizerisches Jahrbuch für Politische Wissenschaft*, 34 (1994): 63–76. I thank the publishers of both for their permission to reproduce these sections.

CONTENTS

CHAPTER 1

═══

From a politics of ideas to
a politics of presence?

In the conventional understandings of liberal democracy, difference is regarded as primarily a matter of ideas, and representation is considered more or less adequate depending on how well it reflects voters' opinions or preferences or beliefs. Problems of political exclusion are perceived either in terms of the electoral system (which can over-represent certain views and under-represent others), or in terms of people's access to political participation (which has proved particularly skewed according to social class). The personal characteristics of the representatives barely figure in this—except perhaps as an after-the-event grumble about the poor quality of our politicians. Most voters know too little about the candidates to make their talents or virtues the basis for political choice. Most voters, indeed, would query whether these should be a central concern. We might all wish to be represented by people we regard as wiser or more able than ourselves, but, faced with a choice between someone more competent and someone whose views we can share, we usually feel safer in giving our support to the latter. The political party provides us with the necessary shorthand for making our political choice: we look at the label rather than the person, and hope we will not be let down.

Though it might seem rather grandiose to describe this dominance of party politics as a high-minded 'politics of ideas', the description conveys some at least of what is involved in current notions of representation. It suggests a broadly secular understanding of politics as a matter of judgement and debate, and expects political loyalties to develop around policies rather than people. It is not a particularly serious qualification to this to note that people's political loyalties are shaped by the communities in which they are born or live, or to recognize that people can 'inherit' attachments to a party that no longer seems consonant with the nature of their lives. Nor is it a particularly serious qualification to note that we give our support to those parties that fit better with our interests, for only the most detached understanding of political ideas would separate these from all aspects of material existence.

A better point of contrast would be with conditions in which party programmes become virtually irrelevant, where politics has been reduced to a stitching together of group-based support, or where votes are 'bought' by material favours. One might think here of the abuse of kinship networks and ethnic solidarities by political élites in post-colonial Africa, many of whom evacuated the terrain of contested policies and ideas to cultivate power bases around exclusionary identities. When the colonial powers retreated from Africa, they left behind them societies in which the state had become the main avenue for economic and social advancement, and where an alternative politics of patronage was almost doomed to flourish. In such contexts, people lived under what seemed an absence of politics, with the contrast between a civilian or a military regime seeming of far less consequence than whether you had access to any of the rulers. As ethnic connections emerged as one of the main routes of access, ethnic rivalries became quite literally deadly, and it is against this sombre background that African writers have so eloquently called for a politics based on vision or ideas.[1]

Which is not to say that all is well, or regarded as such, in the more established liberal democracies. Radical democrats, particularly those of more utopian bent, have continued to explore alternative avenues of 'typical' or 'mirror' or 'random' representation, which they have seen as a better approximation to the old dream of being ruler and ruled in turn, or as a more satisfactory way of ensuring that all interests are adequately addressed. John Burnheim, for example, has suggested that our interests are better protected when we are represented by those who share our experience and interests, and that this similarity of condition is a far better indicator than whether people might share our rather shaky opinions.[2] He proposes a sweeping alternative to electoral politics, in which decision-makers

---

[1] Novels and essays by Chinua Achebe, for example, or Wole Soyinka.
[2] J. Burnheim, *Is Democracy Possible?* (Cambridge, 1985).

would be chosen by lot as a 'statistically representative' sample of the various groups concerned in the decisions. In *A Citizen Legislature*, Callenbach and Phillips also argue for representatives to be chosen by lot rather than elections, with the emphasis on ensuring that these representatives are a typical sample of the various interests spread across the society.[3] Choosing representatives on the basis of their beliefs or opinions (or, more strictly, which party they represent) is often seen as encouraging a mere façade of serious discussion, behind which the people with the money or the access to the media will make sure they get re-elected. This is not necessarily the best way to protect minority interests, nor does it particularly encourage citizens to deliberate on political affairs.[4]

It is with this last in mind that James Fishkin has turned to random sampling as a way of combating the media-circus that surrounds the selection of presidential candidates in the USA. He suggests that a random sample of the voting-age population should be taken off for several days' discussion with and about the different candidates, and that this, combined with what he calls deliberative opinion polls, could inject a more serious note into the selection process.[5] The jury principle would then apply to a wider range of democratic institutions, involving a cross-section of the community and giving them the time to think about the issues at hand.[6]

Despite such occasional incursions into new (or older) territory, most political theorists have been happy to stand by the arguments Hanna Pitkin wielded nearly thirty years ago against mirror or descriptive representation. In particular, they have shared her perception that an over-emphasis on who is present in the legislative assemblies diverts attention from more urgent questions of what the representatives actually do. 'Think of the legislature as a pictorial representation or a representative sample of the nation, and you will almost certainly concentrate on its composition rather than its activities.'[7] Yet representatives, Pitkin argues, are supposed to act, for

---

[3] E. Callenbach, and M. Phillips, *A Citizen Legislature* (Berkeley, 1985).

[4] For a more general discussion of the lottery principle, see B. Goodwin, *Justice By Lottery* (London, 1992).

[5] J. Fishkin, *Democracy and Deliberation: New Directions for Democratic Reform* (New Haven, 1991).

[6] For an earlier discussion of this, see J. Abramson, 'The Jury and Democratic Theory', *Journal of Political Philosophy*, 1/1 (1993).

[7] H. Pitkin, *The Concept of Representation* (Berkeley, 1967), 226.

what would be the point of a system of representation that involved no responsibility for delivering policy results? In her preferred alternative, it is the activities rather than the characteristics that matter, and what happens after the action rather than before it that counts. Representing 'means acting in the interests of the represented, in a manner responsive to them'.[8] Fair representation cannot be guaranteed in advance; it is achieved in a more continuous process, which depends on a (somewhat unspecified) level of responsiveness to the electorate. The representatives may and almost certainly will differ from those they act for, not only in their social and sexual characteristics, but also in their understanding of where the 'true' interests of their constituents lie. What renders this representative is the requirement for responsiveness. 'There need not be a constant activity of responding, but there must be a constant condition of responsive*ness*, of potential readiness to respond.'[9]

Radicals may challenge this resolution as allowing too much independence of judgement and action to the representatives, but the direction their criticisms take also lends little support to proposals that focus on who the representatives are. The most radical among them will scorn what they see as a reformist preoccupation with the composition of political élites. Others will give serious consideration to changes that make existing assemblies more representative of the population as a whole, but they will prefer mechanisms of accountability that minimize the significance of the individuals elected. The shift from direct to representative democracy has shifted the emphasis from *who* the politicians are to *what* (policies, preferences, ideas) they represent, and in doing so, has made accountability to the electorate the pre-eminent radical concern. We may no longer have much hope of sharing in the activities of government, but we can at least demand that our politicians do what they promised to do. The quality of representation is then thought to depend on tighter mechanisms of accountability that bind politicians more closely to the opinions they profess to represent. Where such processes are successful, they reduce the discretion and autonomy of individual representatives; in the process, they seem to minimize the importance of who these individuals might be.

[8] H. Pitkin, *The Concept of Representation* (Berkeley, 1967), 209.
[9] Ibid. 233.

These are powerful arguments, and ones that I take very
But, left like that, they do not engage sufficiently with a w
sense of political exclusion by groups defined by their ge
ethnicity or race. Many of the current arguments over dem
revolve around what we might call demands for political presence:
demands for the equal representation of women with men; demands
for a more even-handed balance between the different ethnic groups
that make up each society; demands for the political inclusion of
groups that have come to see themselves as marginalized or silenced
or excluded. In this major reframing of the problems of democratic
equality, the separation between 'who' and 'what' is to be represented, and the subordination of the first to the second, is very much
up for question. The politics of ideas is being challenged by an alternative politics of presence.

The novelty in this is not the emphasis on difference, for notions
of diversity and difference have been central to liberalism from its
inception and to liberal democracy throughout its formation. The
defining characteristics of liberal democracy, as Robert Dahl[10]
among others has clarified, are grounded in the heterogeneity of the
societies that gave it birth. It was the diversity of the citizenry, as
much as its absolute size, that made the earlier (more consensual)
practices of Athenian democracy so inappropriate to the modern
world. Lacking any half-credible basis for seeing citizens as united
in their goals, theorists of liberal democracy took issue with the
homogenizing presumptions of a common good or common purpose, and made diversity their central organizing theme. John Stuart
Mill's famous vacillations over democracy derived from a double
sense of democracy as both impetus and threat to diversity: something that breaks the hold of any single notion of the good life, but
can also encourage a deadening conformity. In more straightfor-
wardly confident vein, George Kateb has presented constitutional
and representative democracy as that system *par excellence* that
encourages and disseminates diversity. The procedures of electoral
competition do not merely chasten and circumscribe the powers of
government. By promoting a more sceptical attitude towards the
basis on which competing claims are resolved, they also cultivate 'a
general tolerance of, and even affection for diversity: diversity in

[10] R. Dahl, *Democracy and its Critics* (New Haven, 1989).

itself, and diversity as the source of regulated contest and competition'.[11]

Difference is not something we have only just noticed. What we can more usefully say is that difference has been perceived in an overly cerebral fashion as difference in opinions and beliefs, and the resulting emphasis on the politics of ideas has proved inadequate to the problems of political exclusion. The diversity most liberals have in mind is a diversity of beliefs, opinions, preferences, and goals, all of which may stem from the variety of experience, but are considered as in principle detachable from this. Issues of political presence are largely discounted, for when difference is considered in terms of intellectual diversity, it does not much matter who represents the range of ideas. One person may easily stand in for another; there is no additional requirement for the representatives to 'mirror' the characteristics of the person or people represented. What concerns us in the choice of representative is a congruity in political beliefs and ideals, combined perhaps with a superior ability to articulate and register opinions. Stripped of any pre-democratic authority, the role of the politician is to carry a message. The messages will vary, but it hardly matters if the messengers are the same. (Those who believe that men have a monopoly on the political skills of articulating policies and ideas will not be surprised that most messengers are men.)

Once difference is conceived, however, in relation to those experiences and identities that may constitute different kinds of groups, it is far harder to meet demands for political inclusion without also including the members of such groups. Men may conceivably stand in for women when what is at issue is the representation of agreed policies or programmes or ideals. But how can men legitimately stand in for women when what is at issue is the representation of women *per se*? White people may conceivably stand in for those of Asian or African origin when it is a matter of representing particular programmes for racial equality. But can an all-white assembly really claim to be representative when those it represents are so much more ethnically diverse? Adequate representation is increasingly interpreted as implying a more adequate representation of the different social groups that make up the citizen body, and notions of 'typical' or 'mirror' or 'descriptive' representation have then returned with

[11] G. Kateb, 'The Moral Distinctiveness of Representative Democracy', *Ethics*, 91/3 (1981), 361.

renewed force. This time they have the added attraction of appearing severely practical. Contemporary concerns over fair representation often translate into immediately achievable reforms, as with the quota systems that have been adopted by a number of European political parties to deliver gender parity in elected assemblies, or the redrawing of boundaries around black-majority constituencies to raise the number of black politicians elected in the USA. This is not the world of mind-stretching political utopias, but one of realistic—often realized—reforms.

The precursor to this politics was the movement for the 'representation of labour', which swept across the fledgling democracies of Europe in the late nineteenth and early twentieth centuries, and created what are today's labour or social democratic parties. The representation of labour was often a shorthand for two, potentially contradictory, notions, one of which looked to the increased representation of working-class men inside the legislative assemblies, the other of which pursued the representation of a labour *interest*, which might be carried by people other than workers themselves. At a time when labour politics held relatively few attractions for those not of labouring origin, the tension between these two was less discernible than it is today. But those involved in socialist and social democratic parties still argued fiercely over the relationship between intellectuals and the 'authentically' working class, some feeling that a socialist politics should privilege the voices and presence of workers, others that class origins or identities should signify less than adherence to socialist ideas.

In *What Is To Be Done*, Lenin offered one classic refutation of the politics of presence, and the basic premiss of his argument came to be widely agreed by people who had no time for the rest of his views. Stressing the multiplicity of arenas within which the power of capital was exerted, he argued the limits of an experience that was confined to any one of these, and the overriding importance of strategic links between one set of struggles and another. This privileged the all-seeing intellectual (who might in principle originate from any class position or fraction), the political activist who could look beyond each specific struggle or campaign to fit the various pieces of the jigsaw together. When socialist feminists challenged such arguments in the 1970s, one of the things they noted was that they denied legitimacy to women's self-understandings; another was that they presumed an objectivity on the part of these activists that raised them to a God-like level. As Sheila Rowbotham remarked in her critique of Leninist conceptions of the vanguard party, '[t]he Party is presented as soaring above all sectional concerns without providing any guarantees that this soaring will not be in fact an expression of the particular preoccupations of the group or groups with power within it.'[12] Part of what sustained the development of an autonomous women's movement was the arrogance of those who thought that ideas could be separated from presence.

I

Contemporary demands for political presence have often arisen out of the politics of new social movements, and they all reflect inequalities other than social class. This is an important point of distinction, for as long as social class was regarded as the pre-eminent group inequality, arguments could divide relatively neatly between the liberal position, which sought to discount difference (we should be equal *regardless* of difference), and the socialist position, which aimed at elimination (we cannot be equal until the class difference has gone). Once attention shifts to forms of group difference that are not so amenable to erasure, these alternatives no longer seem so plausible. Women do not want to change their sex, or black people the colour of their skin, as a condition for equal citizenship; nor do they want their differences discounted in an assimilationist imposition of 'sameness'. The politics around class always led back to those social and economic conditions in which class differences were grounded. Subsequent developments around race or gender or ethnicity lead more directly to the political level.

The politics that characterizes this is determinedly anti-paternalist, and reflects that explosion of self-confident and autonomous organization which developed in the civil rights movement in the USA, and the women's movements of the 1960s and 1970s. The question of who could best speak for oppressed or disadvantaged groups became a central concern within these movements; and in each case, an earlier unity that was premised on shared ideas gave way to alternative

[12] S. Rowbotham, 'The Women's Movement and Organising for Socialism', in S. Rowbotham, L. Segal, and H. Wainwright, *Beyond the Fragments: Feminism and the Making of Socialism* (London, 1979) 61.

unities forged around shared experience. When a political movement sees itself as based on shared ideals and goals (combating racism, securing civil rights, achieving sexual equality), then commitment to these goals seems the only legitimate qualification for membership. But divergence over strategy and objectives soon combined with growing resentment over the organizational dominance of groups already dominant in the wider society to disrupt these earlier unities. This generated a more identity-based politics which stressed the self-organization of those most directly oppressed.

In the subsequent development of feminist politics, the question of who can best speak for or on behalf of another became a major source of tension, for once men were dislodged from their role of speaking for women, it seemed obvious enough that white women must also be dislodged from their role of speaking for black women, heterosexual women for lesbians, and middle-class women for those in the working class. The search for authenticity—or what Kathleen Jones sees as the dead-end pursuit of that experience which will ground one's authority[13]—then makes it difficult for anyone to represent an experience not identical to her own and, taken to this extreme, renders dialogue virtually impossible. Most feminists have resisted this deadening conclusion, but the problems of authenticity rarely propel them back to the purer regions of a politics of ideas. Indeed, recent contributions have reframed the question of authenticity very much in terms of achieving equality of presence. Daiva Stasiulis, for example, criticizes the anti-racist guidelines developed by the Women's Press in Canada which sought to regulate the publication of white authors who had adopted central characters from a non-white culture.[14] Stasiulis notes that the implementation of such guidelines unwisely circumscribes the capacity to write about experiences or cultures other than one's own, and inadvertently confines minority voices to work only with 'minority' issues or culture. But she goes on to argue that the real issue is not who should speak and from what perspective, but how to ensure full and equal access to publishing opportunities for Native women and women of colour.

[13] K. B. Jones, *Compassionate Authority: Democracy and the Representation of Women* (New York, 1993).

[14] D. Stasiulis, ' "Authentic Voice": Anti-Racist Politics in Canadian Feminist Publishing and Literary Production', in S. Gunew, and A. Yeatman (eds.), *Feminism and the Politics of Difference* (Sydney, 1993).

In an article in the same collection, Anna Yeatman discusses an Australian debate over who can legitimately speak about rape or domestic violence within Aboriginal communities, and whether it is appropriate for white feminists to enter what might more properly be seen as an internal debate. She argues that this is less a matter of policing those white women who have dared to contribute to the discussion, and more a matter of ensuring that 'those who would contest our representations . . . are present to undertake the contestation'.[15] The search for 'pure authenticity' is now largely discredited, as much as anything, because each woman can lay claim to a multiplicity of identities, each of which may associate her with different kinds of shared experience. But the inclusion of previously excluded voices, and the changes this implies in political and other institutions, remains a dominant theme.

The greater insistence on group difference reflects what has been an absolute increase in social diversity, arising from recent patterns of global migration. Not that the scale of post-war migration is particularly unprecedented. It hardly compares with the accumulation of people who moved (or were moved) in the course of the Atlantic slave trade, the European settlements of Canada and Australia and Southern Africa, the Irish flight from famine, or the Jewish flight from successive waves of anti-semitism. But the direction of the migration is now more typically from the poorer to the richer regions of the world, and, perhaps more important, it brings together people from many different countries and cultures. Analysing the pattern of population movements in the modern world, Stephen Castles and Mark Miller identify what they see as four major characteristics: the globalization of migration, which means that more countries are affected, and by migrants from more diverse areas of origin; the acceleration of migration, which means that it is growing in volume in all the major regions of the world; the differentiation of migration, which means that each country may simultaneously attract refugees, people seeking shorter-term work opportunities, and people seeking permanent settlement; and the feminization of migration, which marks out current developments from what was previously a more male-dominated move-

---

[15] A. Yeatman, 'Voice and Representation in the Politics of Difference', in Gunew and Yeatman, *Feminism*, 241.

ment.[16] These features are reflected in some of the most over-use terms in contemporary social analysis—mélange, mosaic, patchwork—all of which seek to capture that overlapping multiplicity of ethnicities and religions and cultures.

This multicultural diversity coincides with an equally striking process of homogenization, and the importance currently attached to group difference expresses a complex double dynamic in which people have become more different and yet more the same. Commenting on recent tensions between Quebec and the rest of Canada, Charles Taylor draws attention to this strange irony, that the secession of Quebec from the rest of Canada became a real possibility just when the value differences had been eroded. An earlier contrast between the liberal English and the illiberal, priest-ridden, French (a contrast, Taylor argues, that was already founded on exaggeration) was swept away in 'the liberal consensus that has become established in the whole western world in the wake of World War II';[17] and it was only as Quebec and the rest of Canada were reaching a broader consensus in their political cultures that the tensions between them became so acute. Also commenting on the coincidence of similarity with difference, Castles and Miller note that:

the move towards cultural pluralism corresponds with the emergence of a global culture, which is fed by travel, mass media and commodification of cultural symbols, as well as by migration. This global culture is anything but homogeneous, but the universe of variations which it permits have a new meaning compared with traditional ethnic cultures: difference need no longer be a marker of strangeness and separation, but rather an opportunity for informed choice among a myriad of possibilities. The new global culture is therefore passionately syncretistic, permitting endless combination of elements with diverse origins and meanings.[18]

A similar process can be discerned in current gender relations, for women are demanding recognition as women just at a point in history when their lives are much closer to men's. Women's participation in the labour market has risen to an extraordinary extent, and, even allowing for high levels of sexual segregation in the

---

[16] S. Castles and M. J. Miller, *The Age of Migration: International Population Movements in the Modern World* (Basingstoke, 1993), 8.

[17] C. Taylor, 'Shared and Divergent Values', in R. L. Watts and D. M. Brown (eds.), *Options for a New Canada* (Toronto, 1991), 54.

[18] Castles and Miller, *Age of Migration*, 273.

tructures of all contemporary societies, there has been
convergence in the life-cycles of the two sexes. The
ly over paid employment has been severely dented—in
f the newly industrializing world it is women who fill
, and in much of high-unemployment Europe it is
women who get the new jobs—and, while women continue to dominate the lower paid, less skilled sectors, this inequality is along a
continuum that brings men and women into closer connection. The
attention currently directed to sexual and other kinds of difference
cannot be understood just in terms of an absolute or growing difference. More precisely, it reflects a shift in political culture and claims,
where people who may be significantly *less* different than at some
point in the past come to assert a stronger sense of themselves and
their identities.

II

The resulting emphasis on political exclusion, and what counts
as political inclusion, significantly alters the framework for debates
on political equality. The main achievement of nineteenth- and
twentieth-century democracy was to make citizenship more universal: pulling down, one after another, all those barriers that excluded
women, people with the wrong religion, the wrong skin colour, or
just people with too little property. Subsequent debates have focused
on what else might be necessary—in the shape of more substantial
equalities in our social and economic life—to realize the promise of
democratic equality. Marxism has offered one kind of answer to the
question; post-war social democracy, with its emphasis on the social
and economic conditions for equal citizenship, has offered another;
John Rawls's difference principle, which regards social and economic inequalities as justified only when they work to the maximum
benefit of those who are most disadvantaged, could be said to offer a
third.[19] Though these debates are far from resolved (even in theory,
much less in practice), my main concern is with the more specifically
political mechanisms which associate fair representation with polit-

[19] Rawls does not present it in these terms, but Joshua Cohen makes a good case
for considering the difference principle as required by the democratic conception:
J. Cohen, 'Democratic Equality', *Ethics*, 99 (1989).

ical presence and emphasize changes at the political level: measures, that is, that regard the gender, race, or ethnicity of the representatives as an important part of what makes them representative, and seek some guarantee of equal or proportionate presence.

All such measures insist on deliberate intervention as necessary to break the link between social structures of inequality or exclusion and the political reflection of these in levels of participation and influence. All of them also agree in looking to specifically *political* mechanisms, seeing these as a pre-condition for longer-term social transformation. They take issue, therefore, with the complacencies of a free market in politics, which sees political equality as sufficiently guaranteed by the procedures of one person, one vote. They also challenge the more standard radical alternative, which has focused attention on prior economic or social change. Whatever their differences on other issues, the traditions of revolutionary Marxism and welfare state social reform have tended to converge on a broadly materialist analysis of the problems of political equality, seeing equal political access as something that depends on more fundamental changes in social, economic, and sometimes educational conditions. The current interest in achieving equal or proportionate presence reverses this, focusing instead on institutional mechanisms—its critics would say 'political fixes'—that can achieve more immediate change.

The roots of this reversal lie partly in frustration with what has proved an unbelievably slow process of structural transformation. But political frustration is not new, and people do not normally change direction just because things take so long. The additional impetus comes from the kind of concerns already outlined, which suggest that the range of political ideas and preferences is significantly constrained by the characteristics of the people who convey them. In a more traditional base–superstucture model, we were advised to concentrate first on generating the social conditions for equal citizenship, then to enjoy the political equalization that flows from this. Such an approach treats policy choices as more straightforward than they really are, underestimating the extent to which strategies (even those devised for equality) will reflect the limits of those currently in power. When policies are worked out *for* rather than *with* a politically excluded constituency, they are unlikely to engage with all relevant concerns.

III

Though the importance attached to political presence is a relatively recent phenomenon, there are a number of precursors in the literature of political science which have addressed the political representation of non-class difference. The most influential of these is associated with Arendt Lijphart's theory of consociational or consensual democracy, which focuses on societies divided along a religious or linguistic axis, often both. In such contexts, Lijphart argues, 'majority rule is not only undemocratic but also dangerous, because minorities that are continually denied access to power will feel excluded and discriminated against and will lose their allegiance to the regime'.[20] The defining characteristic of the alternative consensual democracies is that they will distribute executive power and economic resources in proportion to the size of the different communities. It goes without saying that their electoral systems will follow principles of proportional representation, thereby ensuring that political parties are represented in the legislature in proportion to their overall electoral support. More significantly and uniquely, consociational democracies will also establish some element of power-sharing at executive level (a cabinet, for example, composed of leading figures from all the leading parties); will make some provision for minority veto over those issues that are most socially divisive; and will aim at the proportionate distribution of public funds or positions in the civil service between the constituent communities.

In the theorization of these developments, the emphasis is less on what is just and more on what is necessary, with the imperatives of political order always claiming the last word in deciding which forms of democracy are most appropriate. Not that issues of democratic equity are entirely absent: Lijphart repeatedly stresses the unfairness of majoritarianism when it is applied to plural societies, and sees the winner-takes-all practice of simple majority rule as both dangerous *and* undemocratic. The unfairness, however, is always perceived in rhythmic connection with pragmatic considerations of stability, and this limits the range of issues that Lijphart addresses. Consociationalism has most to say about those cleavages that translate into distinct political parties—where Calvinists and Catholics,

[20] A. Lijphart, *Democracies: Patterns of Majoritarian and Consensus Government in Twenty-one Countries* (New Haven, 1984), 22–3.

for example, vote for different parties—and it has proved itself less adept in responding to the later demands for political inclusion.[21] To be recognized as a serious candidate for power-sharing, a group must not only have a strong sense of itself and its interests; it must form its own political party as well. (It would also help if its existence posed a threat to national unity.)

In the relatively rare conditions where women, for example, form their own distinct political party, they might be able to appeal to principles of consociational democracy as a basis for their political claims. Even then they might be unlucky, for no one really expects women to secede. The question Lijphart sets himself is how 'to achieve and maintain stable democratic government in a plural society',[22] and this inevitably focuses his attention on group divisions that are already activated in politics, preferably in party political guise. This barely touches on more recent formulations of political exclusion, where the groups in question are unlikely to form their own parties, and may not yet be organized as significant and powerful blocs. Because consociationalism conceives of pluralism in terms of a division between 'virtually separate subsocieties',[23] it does not deal with the corrosive consequences of marginalization or powerlessness, and the way these can inhibit the self-organization of groups defined outside the dominant norm. The most marginalized can be as marginal in a consociational democracy as they are anywhere else. Neither the theory nor the practice is about equalizing democratic weight.

Theorists of consociationalism have also been less concerned with whether members of one group can *in principle* represent members of another (can a Calvinist speak for a Catholic?) and more consistently focused on the empirical observation that they do not. The corollary of this is that theorists of consociationalism tend to be

---

[21] One qualification to this is that Belgium and the Netherlands—both cited as examples of consociational democracy, and both committed to the proportionate distribution of public funds between different religious communities—proved themselves more ready to address the subsequent claims of Muslim communities than did Britain. See J. Rath, K. Groenendijk, and R. Pennint, 'The Recognition and Institutionalisation of Islam in Belgium, Great Britain, and the Netherlands', *New Community*, 18/1 (1991).

[22] A. Lijphart, *Democracy in Plural Societies: A Comparative Exploration* (New Haven, 1977), 1.

[23] Ibid. 22.

somewhat cavalier about the basis on which group leaders claim to represent 'their' group, and have explicitly condoned the behind-the-scenes manœuvrings in which the various leaders reach their amicable agreements. The most favourable conditions for a stable consociational democracy are those in which the spokespeople for each segment have relatively unchallenged authority—and indeed, in Lijphart's first analysis of the politics of accommodation in the Netherlands, he saw the deferential nature of the political culture as an important ingredient in its success.[24] Commenting on the limited applicability of this model to divisions based around racial or ethnic identity, Brian Barry has noted that these latter are far less likely to throw up a single unquestioned authority with the recognized right to speak for the group.[25] Where communities are organized around religious, or even class, lines of division, leaders can more readily claim an authority over their supporters based on their superior knowledge of group interests and needs. When a group is defined around what each member may perceive as transparently obvious grievances and solutions, this is more likely to generate a number of contested alternatives, and no agreed leaders or élite. The question of who has the legitimacy to speak for or on behalf of the group is then more inherently contested—and consociationalism hardly addresses this issue.

IV

Questions of group difference have also entered into the domain of more normative political theory, where the central preoccupation has been how to be genuinely even-handed between what may be incompatible cultures or traditions or world-views. This is a problem that looms particularly large in contemporary liberalism, for most liberals have taken pride in an over-arching neutrality between different conceptions of the good, and they have been acutely sensitive to accusations that this smuggles in a preference for one good over another. The politics associated with group difference is then widely discussed (or has come to be so, in the course of the last

[24] A. Lijphart, *The Politics of Accommodation: Pluralism and Democracy in the Netherlands* (Berkeley, 1968).
[25] B. Barry,'Political Accommodation and Consociational Democracy', *British Journal of Political Science* 5/4 (1975).

decade), with emphasis on the relationship between individual freedom and the rights of minority groups. Working from a self-
consciously liberal tradition, both Will Kymlicka and Joseph Raz
have endorsed a multicultural recognition of group rights to sustain
group difference, and both have presented this as implied by liberal
principles of freedom and autonomy.[26] Liberalism cannot confine
itself to an exclusively individualist framework, for the very importance that liberals attach to free and autonomous choice is undermined if there is no associated respect for the different cultures in
which people become free. Kymlicka has developed his arguments
primarily in relation to indigenous peoples, and he distinguishes
what he sees as their legitimate claims to group rights *vis-à-vis* the
majority culture from the more contentious claims of free migrants.
Raz is concerned more explicitly with multiculturalism, and his
argument is buttressed by what he sees as the necessary pluralism of
virtues and values, which can never be combined in a single life. To
give one of his simpler and compelling examples, no single person
can simultaneously embody the crucial qualities that make a good
chairperson, which include the ability to reconcile different points
of view, with the eminently desirable attributes of an advocate,
which include single-minded dedication to a cause.[27] In this, as in
more complex examples, the representation of diversity is not just a
sensible accommodation to the requirements of political stability. It
reflects a more humbling recognition that no one group has a
monopoly on virtue.

Kymlicka then stresses the importance of 'cultural context' in
making options available to people, and appeals to this as a basis for
group-differentiated rights that will help sustain threatened minority cultures. Raz argues that 'individual freedom and prosperity
depend on full and unimpeded membership in a respected and flour-
ishing cultural group',[28] and he sees this as a basis for policies that
might range from the right of parents to ensure the education of their
children within their own culture, to the public support for
autonomous cultural institutions. Neither theorist, it should be

[26] W. Kymlicka, *Liberalism, Community, and Culture* (Oxford, 1989) and
Multicultural Citizenship: A Liberal Theory of Minority Rights (Oxford, 1995);
J. Raz, 'Multiculturalism: A Liberal Perspective', *Dissent* (Winter, 1994).
[27] J. Raz, *The Morality of Freedom* (Oxford, 1986), 404.
[28] Raz, 'Multiculturalism', 72.

noted, is promoting what might be described as an 'anything-goes' moral relativism. The argument depends ultimately on the overriding values of freedom and autonomy, and this sets limits to the tolerance of cultural practices or norms. Raz's respect for different cultures is always conditional: one key condition is that all cultures must practice mutual tolerance and respect; another is the 'right of individuals to abandon their cultural group'.[29] Will Kymlicka's conditions are most commonly defined by the requirements of sexual equality—an issue that has become particularly central to these discussions.

The questions then revolve around the relationship between individual and group rights, and the relationship between liberal and illiberal cultures. How, for example, should a liberal democracy deal with groups whose own framework of beliefs is not particularly liberal? If groups are to be strengthened against the pressures that otherwise threaten their disintegration, this potentially strengthens their power over what they may see as recalcitrant members. What then protects the dissident individual, or guarantees her right of exit?[30] What kinds of rights or freedoms or autonomies can be built into the basic consensus of a society and required of all constituent communities? How are these to be justified if they appeal to principles that are not universally shared?

John Rawls's recent work deals extensively with such questions, but what is notable is the way he translates them into yet another version of the politics of competing ideas. The problem he sets himself in *Political Liberalism* is the diversity of 'reasonable comprehensive religious, philosophical, and moral doctrines'[31] (note the emphasis on doctrines), the crucial point being that each of these doctrines can be both comprehensive and reasonable, and that there is no legitimate basis for writing only one of them into the constitution of the state. The task, then, is to establish that 'overlapping consensus' around principles of fairness and justice that all reasonable doctrines can reasonably agree. Rawls notes that his discussion of

---

[29] Raz, 'Multiculturalism', 73.

[30] See C. Kukathas, 'Are There Any Cultural Rights?' *Political Theory*, 20/1 (1992); W. Kymlicka, 'The Rights of Minority Cultures: Reply to Kukathas', *Political Theory*, 20/1 (1992); and C. Kukathas, 'Cultural Rights Again: A Rejoinder to Kymlicka', *Political Theory*, 20/4 (1992), for a debate on right of exit.

[31] J. Rawls, *Political Liberalism* (New York, 1993), 36.

this might be thought to over-emphasize older controversies over religious toleration that arose in the context of the Reformation, and not to engage fully enough with what he terms 'our most basic problems'[32] of race, ethnicity, and gender. He trusts, however, 'that once we get the conception and principles right for the basic historical questions, these conceptions and principles should be widely applicable to our own problems too'.[33] The comment is a rather startling reminder that Rawls conceives of difference primarily in terms of doctrine or belief, and that he has reformulated what are often demands for political presence into a conundrum of fairness and justice.

That said, Rawls is very much concerned with issues of difference, and in particular with the way that differences in power and perspective can distort political judgements. In his initial resolution of this, he envisaged our achieving the necessary even-handedness through an act of imagination: we would think what kind of principles we could all freely accept if none of us knew our own likely position in the social hierarchy, or what we would come most to value as the good things in life. The famous 'veil of ignorance' would remove vested interests from the picture, for if we did not yet know our own likely position or beliefs, we would have no vested interests to defend. If we did not know, for example, whether we were going to end up as atheists or Muslims or Catholics, we would almost certainly go for some principle of religious toleration, or some separation between religion and politics, that we could make compatible with whichever we came to be. We would then come to see tolerance not just as a necessary evil (or what Rawls later calls a 'modus vivendi'), but as a crucial component in a just society.

In this framework, it would be a nonsense to argue for the proportional representation of atheists and Muslims and Catholics in the decision-making assembly: that would defeat the whole logic of the position, which is based on the power of not yet knowing which we might be. So when Rawls later talks of the 'proper representation' of the point of view of free and equal citizens,[34] he does not at all mean that there should be a rough equality of representation between the different groups that make up the society. Indeed, the parties who get together to agree the founding principles of the

---

[32] Ibid. xxviii.   [33] Ibid. xxix.   [34] Ibid. 115–16.

society are not expected to know the content of all the different conceptions of the good that are going to exist within the society, and it
would block them in their deliberations if they did. The emphasis is
on how to achieve an original constitution that can be demonstrably
even-handed and fair; a set of principles that will allow all these
'properly represented' citizens to pursue their as yet unspecified
(except permissible) doctrines. If the composition of the founding
assembly were deliberately rigged to exclude certain groups, this
would presumably count as an illegitimate intrusion of vested interest. But other than that, it is the suspension of knowledge that guarantees equity of treatment, not the presence of all social groups.

The relationship between democracy and justice is, of course,
perennially troubled, and even if we believe that a more democratically constituted assembly will reach more just decisions (because it is
less open to favouritism and bias), we could hardly be confident that
all its decisions will be just. Majoritarianism is notoriously prone to
injustice, particularly where there are permanent majorities,[35] and
even when additional safeguards have been built in to protect
numerical minorities, the mechanisms of democracy never guarantee
the quality of the outcomes. My point, then, is not that explorations
of justice are inappropriate if they proceed in isolation from institutional arrangements, or that there is no more work to be done on the
normative principles that should regulate relationships between different groups. But recent political theory has offered far more interesting material on the content of policy decisions (what kinds of
decisions are just?) than on the processes through which these are
reached. As Iris Young has argued, the preoccupation with end-state
distributions then tends to ignore the power relations that underpin
decision-making arrangements.[36]

Young's work is one major exception to this, and her own exploration of *Justice and the Politics of Difference* has put issues of group
representation more firmly on the political agenda. She takes issue
with the naivety of those who think that even-handed principles of
justice can emerge through some extraordinary act of imagination;
she goes, indeed, considerably further than this, to query the very
status and value of impartiality. A democratic public, she argues,

[35] L. Guinier, *The Tyranny of the Majority: Fundamental Fairness in
Representative Democracy* (New York, 1994), especially ch. 1.
[36] I. M. Young, *Justice and the Politics of Difference* (Princeton, 1990).

'should provide mechanisms for the effective recognition and representation of the distinct voices and perspectives of those of its constituent groups that are oppressed and disadvantaged';[37] failing such mechanisms, the policy outcomes will almost inevitably reflect the preconceptions of the dominant groups. Young has been concerned mainly with the role of oppressed social groups in the formation of public policy (their right, for example, to generate policy proposals which the decision-makers would then be required to take into account), or with their guaranteed access, as members of specific social groups, to some future deliberative assembly;[38] she has not, on the whole, been much interested in modifying the composition of existing élites. As will become clear in Chapter 2, I differ from her in my characterization of the politics of presence, and do not see this as based on any strong notion of 'group representation'. But Young is still the main exception to what is otherwise the dominant trend in normative political theory, where the problems associated with group difference have been conceived primarily in terms of the fair and even-handed principles that should regulate relationships between different groups. Questions of voice or effective power have been far less fully addressed.[39]

V

The notion that fair representation implies proportionate representation according to social characteristics such as ethnicity or gender is a controversial one, and indeed in many ways it is more controversial than its supporters like to suggest. The under-representation of certain categories of people is often so stark that its injustice seems beyond question. When women, for example, occupy a mere 5 per cent of the seats in a legislative assembly, one need only reverse the position of the sexes to demonstrate the democratic deficit. What would men think of a legislature where they were outnumbered nineteen to one? Most well-intentioned observers can be brought to

[37] Ibid. 184.
[38] She focuses on the first in *Justice and the Politics of Difference*; on the second in I. M. Young, 'Justice and Communicative Democracy', in R. Gottlieb (ed.), *Tradition, Counter-Tradition, Politics: Dimensions of Radical Philosophy* (Philadephia, 1994).
[39] Will Kymlicka is a further exception to this; see his exploration of the politics of group representation in *Multicultural Citizenship*, ch. 7.

acknowledge a problem of under-representation, to accept that there is something unsatisfactory in current political arrangements, and in the way assemblies are monopolized by a limited range of people or perspectives. And, once offered a modest range of reforms that would enable more women or more people from ethnic minorities to put themselves forward as political candidates, most of these well-intentioned observers will be happy to give their support.

When the stakes are raised, however, to include more decisive guarantees of political presence, the potential backing often drops away. This is not only (though it may also be) a matter of intellectual dishonesty, for what most good democrats would like is a way of dealing with political exclusion that does not give too much cred-ibility to the group basis on which people are excluded. Where soci-eties are already divided between competing and exclusionary groups, many will accept—just as a matter of pragmatic necessity—that each of these groups has to be accorded some proportionate rep-resentation, or that some form of power-sharing is required. But the fear of encouraging exclusionary and fragmented identities is particularly acute in the wake of the destructive nationalisms of post-communist Europe, and these same people may recoil from strategies that threaten to introduce or intensify divisions that are not yet so serious. Democracies have stumbled along for many decades without addressing the gender or ethnic composition of elected assemblies, and making sex or ethnicity a serious matter of political contestation might then be thought to generate divisions that have not yet proved so deep. Concerns for political stability have been the driving force behind many consociational proposals for power-sharing; the very same concerns can be equally well wielded *against* a politics of presence.

One common objection, then, is that basing politics around dif-ferences of ethnicity or race or gender tends to a 'balkanization' of the polity that undermines social alliance or social cohesion. One of the strengths of the more conventional politics of ideas is that it encourages citizens to focus their attention on the policy differences that divide them. These divisions may themselves be intransigent, but at least they cut across those other axes of division by race or gender or ethnicity, and thereby help secure alliances across different groups. Men can join forces with women to promote policies of sexual equality; white people can join forces with black people to eradicate racial discrimination; Catholics can join forces with Muslims to secure conditions for religious toleration. Too much emphasis on group difference threatens to propel the citizens out of this realm of unifying ideas, and the prospects for cross-group co-operation then become more bleak. A politics that gives increased weight to social identities may block the very alliances that are necessary for change.

The radical resistance to identity-based politics is often expressed in these terms. It surfaces, for example, in arguments over the leadership of anti-racist organizations, and over whether insisting on an all-black executive will damage the conditions for multi-racial action; it also surfaces in the perennial objections from certain groups of socialists to any autonomous organization by women. A more conservative version stresses the potential threat to national unity when too much weight is given to sub-national forms of identity. This runs through critiques of the 'hyphenated identities' that have flourished in American politics; it also underpins the surprisingly strong resistance of the French educational authorities when Muslim schoolgirls expressed their relatively modest wish to cover their heads in class. It is tempting to respond to such anxieties by saying that identity-based politics already exists; that it is hardly relevant whether we approve it, for it is here whether we like it or not. But since the point of this book is to explore changes in the nature of political representation that would further enhance the significance of race or ethnicity or gender, this is hardly enough of an answer. The politics of presence does attach substantially more weight to group difference than is allowed in the politics of ideas, and the potential consequences of this have to be taken into account.

A second major objection is that making representation even partially dependent on personal or group characteristics seems to undermine the basis for political accountability. Most of us can get to grips with the idea that representatives represent us because of a congruity in political opinions or beliefs, and, however disenchanted we may have become with existing mechanisms of accountability, we have some general sense of how this can or should be developed. What are the comparable mechanisms of accountability through which we can see our representatives as 'representing' us in our capacity as women, or as members of an ethnic or racial minority? Does this move rely on an implausible essentialism which presumes

that all women have identical interests, or that all black people think
the same way? And if not, in what sense are we more fairly represented when we see our representatives as more like ourselves?
Accountability is always the other side of the coin in any discussion
of representation, and it is hard to conceive of accountability except
in terms of policies and programmes and ideas. What then is added
by an additional insistence on equal numbers of women and men, or
a fairer balance between ethnic groups?

A third objection comes from those who have queried the sordid
self-interest of a politics that merely aggregates votes, and have
looked to a more deliberative democracy that could generate genuinely common concerns. Superficially, at least, the politics of presence is at odds with what have been major developments in recent
political theory: the revival of civic republicanism; the theorization
of deliberative or communicative democracy; the renewed attack on
interest group politics. Cynthia Ward, for one, insists that group-
based remedies and civic republicanism do not mix; that giving
added legitimacy to groups acts 'like a corrosive on metal, eating
away at the ties of connectedness that bind us together as a nation';[40]
and that any serious critic of interest group factionalism should
reject the 'group-think' implied in this approach. What is most interesting, however, is that she has to argue this against what she perceives as a dangerous accommodation between the ideals of civic
republicanism and the practice of group representation. Despite the
superficial tension, those engaged in the revival of civic republicanism or the exploration of deliberative democracy have not set themselves in total opposition to any politics of presence; indeed, in the
work of Iris Young and Cass Sunstein, there has been an explicit
incorporation of principles of group representation into the framework of deliberative or communicative democracy.[41]

In subsequent chapters I explore these and other objections, all of
which get a good run for their money, though none of them proves
decisive. The cumulative effect, however, is to strengthen what is the
central thesis of this book: that, while the politics of ideas is an inad-

[40] C. V. Ward, 'The Limits of "Liberal Republicanism": Why Group-Based
Remedies and Republican Citizenship Don't Mix', *Columbia Law Review*, 91/3
(1991), 598.

[41] C. Sunstein, 'Preferences and Politics', *Philosophy and Public Affairs*, 20/1
(1991); Young, 'Justice and Communicative Democracy'.

equate vehicle for dealing with political exclusion, there is little to be gained by simply switching to a politics of presence. Taken in isolation, the weaknesses of the one are as dramatic as the failings of the other. Most of the problems, indeed, arise when these two are set up as exclusionary opposites: when ideas are treated as totally separate from the people who carry them; or when the people dominate attention, with no thought given to their policies and ideas. It is in the relationship between ideas and presence that we can best hope to find a fairer system of representation, not in a false opposition between one or the other.

The preliminary task, of course, is to establish the normative basis for any kind of politics of presence. My comments so far have merely set the scene, describing the development of a new politics around presence, indicating its potential divergence from a more established politics of ideas, suggesting that it carries with it a different understanding of representation. None of these yet establishes a case, for what happens rarely coincides with what we want, and even less so with what is just or right. Chapter 2, then, looks at the normative arguments that can be deployed to defend this development, beginning with the possibility that it is required by the key principles of popular control and political equality, but moving beyond this to an alternative justification grounded in existing structures of exclusion. I identify four key arguments, which can be briefly summarized in terms of the importance of symbolic representation, the need to tackle those exclusions that are inherent in the party-packaging of political ideas, the need for more vigorous advocacy on behalf of disadvantaged groups, and the importance of a politics of transformation in opening up the full range of policy options.

Chapters 3 and 4 then explore these normative issues in relation to two major contemporary developments that have invoked a politics of presence: the pursuit of a guaranteed proportion of women among the candidates chosen by political parties; and the pursuit of guaranteed election for minority representatives through re-districting arrangements in the USA. Chapter 5 turns to the complex and multi-layered politics of inclusion that characterizes contemporary Canada, where claims to political presence jostle alongside demands for minority self-government. In this context, the political aspirations of minority or disadvantaged groups seem to point in very different directions, with some looking to a fuller degree of participation in the central decision-making bodies, and others seeking greater autonomy from the central legislature. The politics of presence appears relevant only to one of these demands.

Chapter 6 returns to a more substantial discussion of the relationship between equal or proportionate presence and the growing literature on deliberative democracy. Finally, Chapter 7 pulls together the remaining loose ends in the argument (not always to my entire satisfaction), and places the argument for political presence in the context of larger ambitions for a revitalized democracy. It should be understood throughout that my arguments are not intended as the only recipe for democratic change, for while I regard the exclusion of minority or disadvantaged groups as a particularly damaging failure, I do not expect the resolution of this to deliver everything we could possibly require.

CHAPTER 2

Political equality and
fair representation

One common definition of democracy presents it as a matter of 'simple majority rule, based on the principle "one person, one vote" ': this, indeed was the working definition suggested by Jon Elster in a recent discussion of the relationship between constitutionalism and democracy.[1] For the purposes of his argument, Elster construes the notion of democracy in broad terms: so much so that it includes regimes 'in which, for instance, slaves, foreigners, women, the propertyless or minors are excluded from the electorate'.[2] Outside the purposes of his argument, such a definition is self-evidently limited, failing to address either the composition of the citizen body or the problems associated with simple majority rule. A more useful definition is that supplied by the Democratic Audit of the UK, which identifies popular control and political equality as the two key principles of democracy, and takes these as the benchmark against which to evaluate contemporary democracy.[3] No system can claim to be democratic if it does not recognize the legitimacy of these two goals; and democracies can be located along a continuum depending on how well these principles are realized in their practice.

The first principle of popular control is intrinsic to any notion of democracy. A system is not regarded as democratic just because it proclaims itself as pursuing the needs or interests of the people, for

[1] J. Elster, 'Introduction' to J. Elster and R. Slagstad (eds.), *Constitutionalism and Democracy* (Cambridge, 1988).

[2] Ibid. 2.

[3] This audit has been set up by the Human Rights Centre at the University of Essex in combination with the Charter 88 Trust. For a discussion of its founding principles, see D. Beetham, *Auditing Democracy in Britain*, The Democratic Audit of the United Kingdom, Paper I (Charter 88 Trust, London, 1993).

democracy always implies that the people themselves take some part in determining political decisions. Democracy is not paternalism: it is not only government 'for the people' but government 'by the people' as well. Democracies have varied enormously in the mechanisms through which people get to exercise this influence or control—just as democracies have varied enormously over who gets included in 'the people'—but no conceivable definition could omit some element of popular control.

The basis for this is partly prudential: a reminder that political decisions are not grounded in unquestioned or absolute truth; and that any form of government that cedes authority to some subgroup of the population is likely to generate tyrannical rule. If the art of good government were comparable to the art of captaining a ship (a parallel first suggested by Plato), we might well choose to be ruled by those trained in its founding principles. But, while most of us would prefer to see experts in charge of navigating the oceans or designing aircraft that fly, we do not normally consider politics just as a matter of technical expertise. We have become accustomed, on the contrary, to quite fundamental disagreement over priorities and principles and goals, and this makes us more resistant to the claims of self-appointed 'guardians' who believe they know what is in our best interest. As has already been noted, diversity has become a central organizing theme in the history of liberal democracy: initially the diversity of religious belief, and later the diversity over secular goals. Against a background of disagreement and difference, popular control is then partly a precautionary measure, grounded in healthy scepticism towards the pretensions of political élites. In its more theorized versions, the argument stresses the fundamental fallibility of human reason;[4] in common-sense formulations, that no one can know better than I do what are my preferences and priorities and needs.[5]

Popular control is also, however, thought to have an independent value, and this links it with the second principle of political equality. Consider here the arguments for universal suffrage, which are only partially grounded in the dangers of tyrannical rule. It is not, on the whole, thought relevant to the case that the interests of women or

---

[4] See B. Barber, *Strong Democracy* (Berkeley, 1984), ch. 3.
[5] This forms an important basis to Robert Dahl's defence of democracy; see his *Democracy and its Critics* (New Haven, 1989).

between political participation and gender. Too many fe[...] perhaps, have repaid the inattention with interest, and have [...] exclusively on the over-participation of men without exploring [...] tional class or racial dimensions. But in either case, political equa[...] has been taken as implying a rough equality in levels of political p[...] ticipation. Significant deviations from this have been treated as caus[...] for concern.

This is not to say that everyone must be equally enthralled by the political process: the interest in politics is unevenly distributed, as is the interest in sport or in jazz; and a free society is usually thought to imply a freedom not to engage in politics.[9] We certainly cannot assume that a society is undemocratic just because its citizens are bored by its politics. But where levels of participation and involvement have coincided too closely with differences by class or gender or ethnicity, this has been taken as prima facie evidence of political inequality, even without further investigation of where this imbalance might lead.

When Sidney Verba and Norman Nie wrote up their major studies of political participation—the first in America, the second in a seven-nation comparison[10]—they took it almost as axiomatic that inequality in participation meant inequality in political influence; and their careful documentation of bias in participation contrasted with a more casual set of assertions about the effects this bias might have. What they discovered was a consistent skewing of participation in favour of those from the higher social classes, with some minor corrective to this when the less advantaged were organized on a group basis. This participatory bias was then said to give the political advantage to those who were already better off, though the bulk of the evidence for this derived from some survey responses suggesting that the actives and inactives had a different set of preferences and priorities, combined with Lord Lindsay's observation that only the wearer of the shoe will know if it pinches.[11]

Fifteen years later, Geraint Parry, George Moyser, and Neil Day

[9] G. Parry, G. Moyser, and N. Day, *Political Participation and Democracy in Britain* (Cambridge, 1992), 416.

[10] S. Verba and N. N. Nie, *Participation in America: Political Democracy and Social Equality* (New York, 1972); S. Verba, N. N. Nie, and J. Kim, *Participation and Political Equality: A Seven Nation Comparison* (Cambridge, 1978).

[11] Verba *et al.*, *Participation and Political Equality*, 301–7.

---

black people might be better served by an enlightened despotism composed of nice white men. Those who argued for universal suffrage certainly contested the validity of such claims, and they had plenty of evidence to hand to demonstrate that under such conditions the interests of women or black people were not well served. But the real substance of their case lay elsewhere, and did not depend on calculating the consequences. In contemporary theories of democracy, the prudential (or negative) case always combines with a more positive assertion of the equal capacity for self-determination, and the equal value that should then be given to all in deciding the issues that affect their lives.

This second principle has become particularly definitive in the development of modern democracy, for, while the roughly equal capacity for reason is more a matter of faith than of empirical confirmation, it translates into what Dahl calls a 'roughly equal qualification'[6] for government. The burden of proof then shifts to those who want to argue for exceptions—and where such proofs are attempted they typically involve the notion that certain categories of people are more like children than adults. This infantilization of entire sections of the adult population has become increasingly hard to swallow, and, while people continue to disagree about the age at which children turn into adults, their arguments about those who are obviously adult move within a more bounded range than before. There are not many who will now declare themselves as opposed to women's right to vote, and, while plenty can be found who would like to see off their country's ethnic or racial minorities, hardly anyone will argue for two classes of citizenship, defined by the colour of one's skin. People differ substantially in their attitudes to immigration, to policies of multiculturalism, or to what is an appropriate division of labour between women and men. But they do not differ much over the equal rights of those now recognized as citizens, or the equal weighting that should be given to each. The kind of plural voting that John Stuart Mill proposed as an antidote to the idiocies of mass democracy is not at all popular today. Extra votes for college graduates have definitely gone out of fashion, and so too have the overtly discriminatory literacy tests that kept so many black Americans off the electoral register. Whatever else we disagree on—

[6] Ibid. 97.

and there is little sign of consensus on matters of social or economic equality—political equality between adults has come to set the terms for modern democracy.

On the face of it, at least, these two principles of popular control and political equality provide a good basis for the politics of presence. Control is just a pious aspiration unless people are actually there; equality is hardly achieved when some groups have so much more leverage than others. It would be comforting to leave it at that (and would save both reader and writer from much additional work), but this easy deduction is hampered by two major preliminary problems. The first relates to the status of representative democracy, and the way this has changed the conditions for popular control. In the framework of direct democracy, control is a function of presence; for the capacity to influence political decisions depends quite simply on attendance at the relevant meetings, and those not present at the meeting lose their chance of exerting control. But the development of representative institutions has fundamentally altered this equation—has changed it, indeed, quite deliberately, in order to cope with the enlarged citizenry of the modern state. Does this development then undermine the importance of political presence, detaching it from the conditions for popular control?

The second set of problems relates to the status of political equality, a term so slippery in its implications that Charles Beitz, for one, wishes we could drop it from our vocabulary altogether.[7] One standard formulation of political equality is that 'everyone should count for one, and none for more than one'; compared with 'some people should count for more than the others', this looks self-evidently right. The appealing simplicity is, as always, deceptive. 'Count for one' sounds like a broadly procedural matter, to be achieved by ensuring that each individual carries the same voting weight as the next. But what of those individuals who form a permanent minority, whether in their constituency or in the society as a whole? What if their preferences are always discounted, because they happen to vote in the wrong place? Does counting equally refer only to our starting positions, or does it extend to our influence on outcomes? Does the emphasis on individual equalities also extend to equalities between social groups? As arguments about electoral systems amply confirm,

[7] C. R. Beitz, *Political Equality: An Essay in Democratic Theory* (Princeton, 1989).

political equality can lend itself to a wide range of interpretations, some of which focus on equalizing the size of different voting constituencies, others on equalizing the probability that each voter will cast the deciding vote, others still on ensuring that each voter has equal influence on the composition of the government elected.[8] If political equality is itself so indeterminate, how could it be the basis for anything as provocative as a politics of presence?

In the following two sections I explore these questions in more detail, and argue that the case for political presence cannot be viewed as a transparent deduction from either popular control or political equality. These two principles certainly set the framework for any politics of presence, but the core of the argument lies in a more historically specific analysis of existing structures of exclusion and existing arrangements for representation. The central sections then set out these arguments, which can be briefly summarized in terms of the importance to be attached to symbolic recognition, the need to tackle those exclusions inherent in the party packaging of political ideas, the need for more vigorous advocacy on behalf of disadvantaged groups, and the importance of a politics of transformation in opening up a fuller range of policy options. In the final sections, I address the status of experience as an alternative 'guarantee', and take issue with the essentialism implied in this.

I

The first issue is best approached by considering the differences between political participation and political representation, for, while equality of presence is already implicit in the former, it is not so obviously implicit in the latter. The literature on democracy and participation takes as its starting point the notion that political equality involves some degree of equality in participation, and it treats the systematic absence of particular social groups as a self-evident failing of democracy. The literature varies, of course, in the groups it considers worthy of attention. Numerous political scientists have pondered the disturbing correlations between social class and levels of political participation, but many of these passed over without comment what have been equally disturbing correlations

[8] J. Still, 'Political Equality and Election Systems', *Ethics*, 91/3 (1981).

were noticeably more circumspect in saying why inequalities in participation might matter, stressing only the 'plausibility' of the argument that democracy is 'adversely affected' when those who are active are highly unrepresentative of the population as a whole, and the general likelihood that, when 'certain groups or classes are consistently more active than others, the élites are in some danger of mistaking the pressures of these groupings for the views of the citizenry as a whole'.[12] These cautious words might suggest that inequality in participation is not such a serious concern, but it is equally legitimate to view them in the opposite light. Participatory equality—in the sense of a rough equality between all relevant social groupings—has entered sufficiently deeply into our understandings of democracy to stand almost independently of what we might later discover are its political effects. If subsequent scrutiny established that an under-participation of women or an over-participation of the middle classes had no observable consequences (an unlikely outcome, but still in principle possible), this would not significantly alter the judgement that such inequality is undesirable. Empirical information about actual consequences is regarded as largely beside the point.

The same presumption does not, however, operate in the sphere of representation, and those who see political equality as implying a roughly proportionate distribution of political activity rarely extend the argument to this higher realm. There is no comparable expectation of equality when it comes to the distribution of people on representative bodies—and there is some basis for this differential treatment. Representation is not, after all, just another aspect of participation, to be judged by identical criteria. The activities we group together under the rubric of political participation are ones that every citizen could, in principle, do. We could all vote in the election, and indeed in some countries this is compulsory. We could all sign the petition; we could all turn up at the meeting (though the organizers would not know where to put us if we did); we could all join a political party (though political parties would lose their meaning if we all chose to join the same one). Everyone could in principle be present, and it is a relatively easy step from that to the notion that those who do turn up or out ought to be a representative sample of

---

[12] Parry *et al.*, *Political Participation*, 416.

the population as a whole. There is no such ease of transition in relation to representation, which has been built on the opposite principle of choosing some few to represent the rest.

Equality of presence—a rough approximation to the social groups that make up the society—is already implicit in the notion of participation. It is not so obviously implicit in the notion of representation, which was, if anything, dreamt up to get round this bothersome condition. The two are related, and a society that provided genuinely equal access to participation in meetings and pressure groups and parties would almost certainly produce the same kind of equality among the people elected. In principle, however, they are distinct, for, in distancing itself from participatory democracy, representative democracy has distanced itself from physical presence as the measure of political equality. As applied to political participation, it might seem entirely appropriate that those who are most active should in some way mirror the composition of the population as a whole. There is no such compelling reason when it comes to representation.

This is indeed the burden of Hanna Pitkin's critique of mirror or descriptive representation. In her influential work on *The Concept of Representation*,[13] she suggested that the metaphors of descriptive representation were most commonly found among those who regarded representative democracy as a poor second-best, and who therefore looked to more 'accurate' or pictorial representation of the electorate as a way of approximating the older citizen assemblies. Instead of recognizing the qualitatively new element that entered into democracy with the development of representative institutions, these defiant romantics continued to pursue criteria that were more appropriate to an earlier age. In the 1780s debates on the American Constitution, for example, Federalists and anti-Federalists differed not only on the appropriate division of power between federal and state government but also in their understanding of what it was to 'represent'. In this context (as in many others), the Federalists were the modernizers who had more fully grasped the spirit of their time. As Edmund Morgan puts it, they saw representative democracy as superior to direct democracy precisely because it 'enabled the people to delegate power to persons as unlike most of themselves as possible, to persons distinguished by their abilities and talents, by the

[13] H. Pitkin, *The Concept of Representation* (Berkeley, 1967).

very talents that would lead voters to favour them'.[14] The best political leaders would then inspire by their integrity and merit, and they would be people who could see more widely and deeply than those whose future they were chosen to guide. The anti-Federalists had little confidence in this—partly, of course, because they knew they would not dominate the federal assembly—and they were deeply agitated by what they saw as the dangers of remote government. They included in this not just the remoteness of federal government, but the growing gap between representatives and people. Hence their preference for state over federal assemblies, but hence also their support for more frequent elections and their attempts to ensure some rotation in office. 'They accepted the unfeasibility of direct democracy, but they regretted its unfeasibility and wanted government to resemble it as closely as possible by making the few who governed resemble in every way the many they governed.'[15]

Given the subsequent divergence between direct and representative democracy, the politics of presence might well appear as a curious replay of that earlier, now outmoded, debate. The equal right to participate is a natural enough extension of the equal value allocated to all citizens, and any deviations from rough proportionality do then seem to give legitimate cause for concern. Taking such deviations seriously already raises controversial questions about the relationship between formal and substantial equality. (Is it enough to give people formal equalities, or do we also need to address the structural obstacles that prevent certain groups from making full use of their equal rights?) But as long as the emphasis is on political *participation*, the argument moves within relatively well defined territory inherited from the practices of direct democracy. Representation, has however, significantly altered the political terrain, and a proportionality that might have been quite appropriate in previous contexts no longer seems such a major concern. As Pitkin has quite adequately established, the equation of fair representation with proportionate representation follows from only one among many versions of what representation is about. And while that particular version may be perfectly legitimate, it cannot be said to

---

[14] E. S. Morgan, 'Power to the People?' *New York Review of Books* (2 Dec. 1993), 28.
[15] Ibid. 27.

follow automatically from the equal right to participate in politics. Political equality does carry with it an equal right to participate in politics—an equal right to be politically present. Translating this into an equal right to serve as a representative simply presumes what has yet to be established.

II

The questions raised around representation take us into the second area of ambiguity, which relates to the very meaning of political equality. When it is taken out of historical context, the general aspiration to political equality can give only moderate guidance on the institutions that best meet its requirements. Political equality does not specify just one kind of treatment. It can be taken to mean that all citizens should have equal power over outcomes, that all political preferences should be given equal weight, or (somewhat less plausibly) that all citizens should have an equal chance of voting for a winning candidate. There is no guarantee that these different objectives will coincide, which means we often have to make judgements between them. It may be, for example, that in order to give people equal power over outcomes we have to weight their preferences unequally; or that in order to protect minorities we have to give their votes some additional weight. Simplistic appeals to political equality leave the most difficult questions unanswered, for there is little that flows directly and unequivocably from the meaning of political equality.

Part of what is at issue here is the ambiguous nature of equality: an ambiguity that has been widely rehearsed in feminist explorations of the difference between being treated as equals and being treated as if we are the same.[16] When we think of equality as what Charles Beitz terms a 'simple univocal principle',[17] we turn it into a unique set of prescriptions that must apply regardless of historical context. We then lose the flexibility and sensitivity that enable us to judge between different situations—and we may become baffled by the most ordinary of questions. Some feminists in the USA, for example,

---

[16] C. Bacchi, *Same Difference: Feminism and Sexual Difference* (London, 1990); M. Minow, *Making All the Difference* (Ithaca, NY, 1990); G. Bock and S. James, (eds.), *Beyond Equality and Difference* (London, 1993).

[17] Beitz, *Political Equality*, 225.

treats women differently from men. Faced with the prospect of differential legislation that distinguishes—and then potentially discriminates—between the sexes, they have preferred the gender-neutral policies that equate pregnancy with a 'temporary disability', and can apply more even-handedly between women and men.[18] Treating women as different, even in respects in which they *are* patently different from men, has been regarded as too much a hostage to fortune. And yet the solution to this dilemma seems simple enough. In some circumstances equality means differential treatment; in other circumstances it means treating people the same—there is no logical or political requirement to stand by just one of these two options. What prevents people from seeing this is precisely that 'univocal principle' of equality that Beitz criticises: an overly rigid understanding of equality that abstracts it from any meaningful context.

In exploring the forms of democracy most appropriate to an egalitarian society, Ronald Dworkin draws attention to two very different approaches.[19] The first he describes as a *dependent* interpretation of democracy: one that makes the choices over mechanisms and procedures depend on the kinds of outcomes they are likely to produce and, more specifically, on whether they will treat all members of the community with equal concern. The alternative, *detached*, interpretation tests things by input rather than output, conceiving of democracy as the equal distribution of power over political decisions. Though this is the version that lies behind most common-sense understandings of democracy as 'one person, one vote'—and is by far the more favoured approach—it is, in Dworkin's view, incoherent. Equal power must be taken to imply equal influence (otherwise there is no basis for criticizing the unfair influence of wealthier citizens); but equal influence can be achieved only by eliminating politics itself. As long as people are allowed to act, some will have more influence than others, if only by virtue of their personal charisma or their greater experience in political argument and debate. The more controversial emphasis on equality of outcomes then emerges as

---

[18] These debates may seem odd from a European context, where maternity leave has long been part of a welfare agenda, but they have perplexed and divided feminists in the USA. See Z. Eisenstein, *The Female Body and the Law* (Berkeley, 1989).

[19] R. Dworkin, 'What is Equality? 4: What is Political Equality?' *University of San Francisco Law Review*, 22 (1988).

stronger than it initially seemed, and Dworkin argues for a dependent interpretation of democracy that can take account of consequences as well as original conditions.

Charles Beitz addresses a similar range of issues when he considers the tension between establishing an equal power over outcomes and achieving an equal weighting of political preference. The first concentrates on the input (get the procedures right and leave the results to themselves), while the second deals with the output (are citizens treated fairly in the policy results?). In any legitimate understanding of democracy, both must surely be taken into account. 'Citizens must be treated equally as participants in the political process; but they must also be treated equitably as the subjects of public policy.'[20] Beitz then argues for what he terms 'complex proceduralism', in which fair terms for participation are determined by what can be made justifiable to each citizen in the light of both aspects of equal treatment. This moves us away from absolute notions of equality, which hold for all time and all place, and may be thought to legitimate what is currently believed or accepted rather than what is independently 'right'.[21] But we cannot deduce what is politically fair from abstract principles of political equality: we have to draw on empirical judgements of what is likely to happen as well as what seems in principle to be fair.

Both arguments note the ambiguity at the heart of political equality, and both clarify the role of consequentialist considerations in determining what counts as fair and just. The case for equal or proportionate presence cannot be derived simply from general principles of political equality; but neither can the case against. We have to look at how political representation works in existing conditions, and whether arrangements that might seem to embody general principles of fairness none the less favour particular groups. The politics of ideas takes its stand on abstracting from social difference; the political influence we wield will depend on how many others we persuade to adopt our particular beliefs. What are the alternative arguments that provide the basis for a politics of presence?

---

[20] Beitz, *Political Equality*, 155.   [21] Ibid. 225–6.

III

The under-representation of certain categories of people is in one sense just empirical fact: they are not present in elected assemblies in the same proportions as they are present in the electorate. But the characteristics of those elected may diverge in any number of ways from the characteristics of those who elect them, and this is not always seen as a matter of democratic consequence. In a much cited article on representation, A. Phillips Griffiths argued that some divergences are regarded as positively beneficial. We do not normally consider the interests of lunatics as best represented by people who are mad, and 'while we might well wish to complain that there are not enough representative members of the working class among Parliamentary representatives, we would not want to complain that the large class of stupid or maleficent people have too few representatives in Parliament: quite the contrary'.[22] Feminists may find the implied parallels unconvincing, especially when they recall the many decades in which women were classified with children and the insane as ineligible for the right to a vote, but the general point remains. Establishing an empirical under-representation of certain groups does not in itself add up to a normative case for their equal or proportionate presence. It may alert us to overt forms of discrimination that are keeping people out, but it does not yet prove the case for more radical change.

It does, however, provide a basis for the first part of the argument for political presence, which relates to what Hanna Pitkin described—and rather speedily dismissed—as symbolic representation. When those charged with making the political decisions are predominantly drawn from one of the two sexes or one of what may be numerous ethnic groups, this puts the others in the category of political minors. They remain like children, to be cared for by those who know best. However public-spirited their mentors may be, this infantilization of large segments of the citizenry is hardly compatible with modern-day democracy, and it becomes particularly burdensome when associated with popular ideologies that have presumed the inferiority of the excluded groups. Claims on political representation then figure as one of many avenues for challenging

---

[22] A. Phillips Griffiths, 'How Can One Person Represent Another?' *Proceedings of the Aristotelian Society*, 34 (1960), 190.

existing hierarchies of power; as Lani Guinier puts it in a discussion of black representation in the USA, '[b]lacks cannot enjoy equal dignity and political status until black representatives join the council of government'.[23] Including those previously excluded matters *even if* it proves to have no discernible consequences for the policies that may be adopted. Part of the purpose, that is, is simply to achieve the necessary inclusion: to reverse previous histories of exclusion and the way these constituted certain kinds of people as less suited to govern than the rest.

This more symbolic element in representation is sometimes linked to arguments about making political institutions more legitimate, more obviously and visibly representative of those they pretend to represent. But this is an explicitly pragmatic argument, aimed at the weak spots of those who prefer to keep things as they are. The case for equal or proportionate presence is not, on the whole, about making liberal democracies more stable, or pre-empting the mass alienation of citizens who might otherwise take to the streets. What is at issue, rather, is what Charles Taylor has called the 'politics of recognition'.[24] Because the modern age makes identity more problematic (much less taken for granted), it also makes recognition far more important to people's well-being; and if your way of life is not recognized as of equal value with others, this will be experienced as a form of oppression. The required recognition has been widely interpreted as including a more public presence in political life: a public acknowledgement of equal value.

This first part of the argument could of course be met in other ways than through changing the composition of elected assemblies. If what is required is a public acknowledgment that differences exist, and that all groups are equally part of the political community, this might be better achieved through changing the curriculum in universities or schools, or funding the cultural activities of different social groups, or redesigning the national flag. But the argument for a fuller public presence for those currently marginalized, infantilized, or excluded nearly always carries with it additional expectations about how this will alter the direction of policy or the content

[23] L. Guinier, 'Keeping the Faith: Black Voters in the Post-Reagan Era', *Harvard Civil Rights–Civil Liberties Law Review*, 24 (1989), 421.
[24] C. Taylor, 'The Politics of Recognition', in A. Gutmann (ed.), *Multiculturalism and the 'Politics of Recognition'* (Princeton, 1992).

of the decisions that are made. It is at this point, rather than in the emphasis on public recognition, that it more directly challenges existing notions of representation.

IV

That representation is a muddle is accepted by most political theorists. If we could transport ourselves into a simpler political universe where citizens had only two choices (say, between tending the fields or preparing the country for war), then, assuming a reasonably satisfactory electoral system and representatives who do what they say, the outcome would reflect majority feeling, and the democratic process would be nicely assured. But not only do we doubt the integrity of our representatives and the transparency of our electoral systems, we also know there are more than two choices that will have at some point to be made. The way these get packaged by the different political parties already introduces one element of difficulty, for we may like what one party proposes on health provision, but prefer what another says on education. And even when we work out some rule of thumb for deciding which issues most matter, what of all the other choices that did not even appear on the political agenda? The importance of these may not become apparent until long after the election, and it will then be too late to pass on any message about what we would prefer our representatives to do.

At this point, we can of course resort to the various contacting, campaigning, and pressure group activities which enable citizens to pass on their preferences in the gap between the elections. But most commonly, we fall back on the vague expectation that representatives who share our views on one set of issues will share our views on another set too. It hardly needs saying that this expectation makes most sense when politics is organized around binary oppositions, or when political beliefs and objectives fall into coherent clusters of congruent ideas. When class was the central organizing principle defining a left–right political spectrum, this presumption looked more plausible than it does today. But positions on the ownership of the means of production or the distribution of income and wealth were never very good predictors of positions on sexual or racial equality; and nor were positions on sexual equality such good predictors of attitudes on class or race. The American suffragists who campaigned for women's right to vote often arrived at their commitment through what they saw as a parallel involvement in campaigns against black slavery; but many of them later opposed the enfranchisement of black men as a further obstacle to women's inclusion. Several years later, British suffragists found some of their strongest supporters as well as their most obdurate opponents within the ranks of socialist men, many of whom perceived the obsession with women's equality as a dangerously middle-class diversion from the more pressing concerns of class. Political positions on these most fundamental aspects of social and political equality do not necessarily coincide; political positions on lesser matters can be even more diverse.

The example of the suffrage movement makes it clear that politics never did fit a single 'left–right' spectrum, and that the compulsory packaging of what can be very diverse goals or beliefs never did much justice to their subtlety or range. The often binary alternatives have, however, become particularly inappropriate to the complexity of contemporary identity and belief, and the declining salience of class is best understood in this context. It is not that problems of class inequality and deprivation are any less pressing than before, but that class can no longer operate as the organizing symbol for such a multiplicity of political concerns. And yet the pattern of representation that is most characteristic of contemporary liberal democracies still assumes that beliefs and concerns can be packaged in relatively straightforward ways—and, in many instances, into only two parcels.

In most parts of the liberal and social democratic world, there is just enough congruity between different kinds of issues for this to retain some rough plausibility. (If there were *no* such connection, political parties could hardly exist in their current form.) Thus, parties on the left and centre of what is still a largely class-defined political spectrum have tended to take the initiative in introducing measures for women's social and political equality; these same parties have also tended to be more responsive to the claims of multiculturalism or the demands of ethnic minorities. There is, to that extent, some semblance of a connection between different kinds of issues. But no one studying the history of policies on immigration or the development of apartheid in South Africa would end up overly optimistic on the convergence of interests between differently subordinated groups; just as few of those comparing the history of liberal and socialist traditions would find themselves in total and consistent agreement with only one of these two.

The lack of fit between different sets of issues poses a major problem for existing conventions of representation, and it provides the second part of the argument for a different politics of representation. If we were to be strict in our definitions, we would have to say that representatives only 'really' represent their constituents on the issues that were explicitly debated in the course of the election campaign. On everything else, the representatives have to fall back on their own judgement or their own prejudice. And though some of this could be averted by fuller discussion of a wider range of issues, citizens have neither the time nor the knowledge to extract a comprehensive statement of what candidates might think on every issue that might conceivably arise. They then have to fall back on some more general notion of the ways in which they are being represented. Failing that more innocent political spectrum which would enable them to predict views on abortion from views on nuclear defence, they have to turn to other aspects of the candidates which might serve as a complementary protection. Whether these candidates are male or female, black or white, recent or long-ago migrants, can then become of major significance.

This edges into the third argument for changing patterns of representation, which is that people from disadvantaged groups need more aggressive advocates on the public stage. Not that people never act for anyone other than themselves: some of the existing political parties have established a worthy record of policies against discrimination or programmes for disadvantaged groups; and wherever such policies are implemented, it is by legislative assemblies in which those discriminated against have a negligible presence. Politicians are elected on party commitments, which might include any number of policies relating to sexual or racial equality or the fairer treatment of minority groups. If there is a clear mandate for these policies, does it really matter who the politicians are? Why not put the effort into establishing the commitments, rather than bothering about the characteristics of the people who implement them?

Part of the answer to this refers back to symbolic representation, for there is something distinctly odd about a democracy that accepts a responsibility for redressing disadvantage, but never sees the disadvantaged as the appropriate people to carry this through. The other part is grounded in a rather sober pessimism about the limits to binding mandates. As any reasonably diligent observer of the political process will confirm, policy decisions are not settled in advance by party programmes or election commitments. New problems and issues always emerge alongside unanticipated constraints, and in the subsequent weighing of interpretations and priorities it can matter immensely who the representatives are. When there is a significant under-representation of disadvantaged groups at the point of final decision, this can and does have serious consequences. However strong our attachment to the politics of binding mandates (people of course vary in this), representatives *do* have considerable autonomy, which is part of why it matters who those representatives are.

These arguments then combine with the last, which stresses those ideas or concerns that have not even reached the political agenda. The problem of representation is not just that preferences refuse to cluster around a neat set of political alternatives, or that the enforced choice between only two packages can leave major interest groups without any voice. There is an additional problem of the preferences not yet legitimated, the views not even formulated, much less expressed. As Cass Sunstein has argued, there are serious risks attached to taking political preferences as fixed or finite givens, and one of these is that preferences are always formed in relation to what has been set as a norm.[25] Though many of us will rail against what we see as an unjust allocation of the good things in life, many more of us will adjust our expectations downwards in order to survive and remain sane. People adapt themselves to 'undue limitations in available opportunities or to unjust background conditions',[26] and, as Sunstein notes, 'poverty itself is perhaps the most severe obstacle to the free development of preferences and beliefs'.[27] Those more favoured by fortune may, by the same logic, have exaggeratedly high expectations, and they may far exceed the requirements of justice in what they consider to be theirs by right. If we take the preferences that are expressed through the mechanism of the vote as the final word on what governments should or should not do, we may be condemning large sections of the community to persistently unjust

[25] C. R. Sunstein, 'Preferences and Politics', *Philosophy and Public Affairs*, 20/1 (1991).

[26] Ibid. 4.   [27] Ibid. 23.

conditions. It is no real justification for this to say that it is what people said they wanted.

In the market-place paradigm which sees citizens choosing between packages of political ideas, there is little space for further development. People become consumers of existing products, and cannot do much to alter the range. They can pressure political parties to take up issues that no one party has so far addressed, and once these issues are on the agenda they can use the ballot box to 'punish' those who still ignore them. They may not, however, even be able to formulate these new issues if they are not first drawn into the political process. It is only when people are more consistently present in the process of working out alternatives that they have much chance of challenging dominant conventions. The argument for a more equitable distribution of representative positions is very much bound up with this.

These arguments are the cornerstone for any politics of presence. The first part relates to the symbolic significance of who is present, and the independent importance that has to be attached to including groups that have been previously denied or suppressed. The second and third refer more directly to the policy consequences we can anticipate from changing the composition of elected assemblies. Political preferences do not fall into the neat packages of party politics, and in order to achieve more fair and adequate representation of those interests that were not explicitly consulted or debated during election campaigns, as well as more vigorous advocacy at the moment of final decision, it is vital to achieve that additional element of representation which arises from the presence of previously excluded groups. These first arguments are reinforced by the last, which stresses a politics of transformation. Since all the options are *not* already in play, we need to ensure a more even-handed balance of society's groups in the arenas of political discussion. The social construction of political preference means that some possibilities will have been opened up and other ones closed down, and relying only on what is registered through the vote (through the initial choice of representatives) will then reinforce what is already dominant. If fair representation also implies fair representation of what would emerge under more favourable conditions, we have to address the composition of the decision-making assemblies as well as the equal right to a vote.

V

There are two standard objections levelled at these conclusions, and the first invokes that notorious slippery slope which stretches from women, ethnic minorities, and the disabled to take in pensioners, beekeepers, and people with blue eyes and red hair. Once the characteristics of the people are acknowledged as relevant, there is said to be a potentially endless list of groups that will all claim the same kind of attention, and no legitimate basis for distinguishing between some of these groups and the others. The implication, it hardly needs saying, is that we would do better to keep off the entire terrain.

Though often delineated with deliberately deflationary intent, this supposed chain of connections does have some logic behind it. If fair representation simply *meant* proportional representation, there would be no guiding principle for deciding which things most mattered, and we would soon find ourselves mapping each and every variable, from the most to the least significant. The task would prove beyond us, for not only is there an infinite number of possibilities, but even the most obvious candidates for mapping will be very likely to conflict. Imagine a society in which women were twice as likely as men to support the free-market policies of the Centre–Right Party, and men twice as likely as women to support the environmentally sensitive policies of the Greens. Do we go for the election of two women for every one man as representatives of the first party, and two men for every one woman as representatives of the second? Or do we go for equal numbers within each party, and prioritize gender over gender-plus-beliefs? The absurdities can multiply, but they soon lose their sustenance if we just drop the initial abstraction. Political equality does *not* require proportionality according to each and every characteristic: political equality *per se* cannot settle the outstanding arguments. The case for a different system of representation depends on more historically specific analysis of the existing arrangements for representation and the existing conditions of political inclusion.

This is an important qualification to the arguments for changing the composition of elected assemblies, for, while these draw obvious sustenance from principles of equality and fairness, they do not depend on any simple extrapolation from them. The case for gender parity in politics, or for a more even-handed balance between the different ethnic groups that make up the society, or indeed for a greater than proportionate representation of numerically small groups,[28] always depends on analysis of existing structures of exclusion. It is never simply 'required' by the meaning of political equality or the nature of fair representation. It is representation, that is, with a purpose; it aims to subvert or add or transform. The underlying preoccupation is not with pictorial adequacy—does the legislature match up to the people?—but with those particularly urgent instances of political exclusion which a 'fairer' system of representation seeks to resolve.

It is worth noting, in this context, that, while Charles Beitz remains profoundly sceptical on the general arguments for proportional representation, he gives some moderate backing to the redistricting arrangements that have created what are effectively 'safe seats' for black Americans. He argues this, not on the more general ground of a proportionality that is always and everywhere required, but because there are 'predictable kinds of injustice' that have been built into American history, which provide a more contingent basis for adopting proportional techniques.[29] Iris Young's argument for group representation can be seen to follow a similar pattern. She never suggests that all groups would qualify for additional group representation (beekeepers, Christians, members of the Ku Klux Klan), but argues that those groups that can be identified as oppressed within the wider society need some guaranteed route to public policy-making that will counter their more normal political exclusion.[30] This is not a general argument about fair representation being proportional representation; indeed, in Young's case it is an

[28] Will Kymlicka argues that threshold representation may be more important than proportional representation, and that this could mean more than proportionate representation for groups that are very small and less than proportionate representation for groups like women; see W. Kymlicka, 'Group Representation in Canadian Politics', in F. L. Seidle (ed.), *Equity and Community: The Charter, Interest Advocacy and Representation* (Montreal, 1993).

[29] Beitz, *Political Equality*, 159. It is interesting that Beitz reverses the standard European preference, which has tended to view the proportional representation of political parties with more equanimity than the proportional representation of people by the colour of their skin. This pattern of preference does, of course, mirror American common sense.

[30] I. M. Young, *Justice and the Politics of Difference* (Princeton, 1990). It should be said, however, that her list of oppressed groups threatens to embrace nearly all of America's population. The only ones left out, as Will Kymlicka puts it, are able-bodied young white men.

argument for *more* representation than is strictly proportional to one's numbers.

VI

The second objection recognizes that there is indeed a problem of political packaging, but sees this as more adequately dealt with by measures to ensure the proportional representation of political ideas. 'Who' is present is then redefined as a problem of 'what', and the emphasis shifts to ways of achieving legislative assemblies that will mirror the full range of political preferences as expressed in the popular vote. This then leads into a more technical investigation of the competing merits of the single member, winner-takes-all, systems that operate in Britain or the USA, and those systems of proportional representation that are more common outside the Anglo-American world. These debates have been contentious enough, but they work within a relatively uncontroversial understanding of proportionality as a matter of proportionality to the citizens' ideas.

Many commentators regard this as less problematic than any further matching to characteristics such as gender or ethnicity: partly because it is already practised in a majority of contemporary democracies (what already happens rarely seem very contentious); partly because it seems less socially divisive; partly because it is more in keeping with the dominant politics of ideas. In the debates around the new constitution for South Africa, for example, a system of proportional representation for political parties was widely supported as a way of achieving proportionality between the different ethnic groups without actually specifying ethnic 'rights' to office. 'Ethnicity must not be rewarded politically', as Gerhard Maré has put it,[31] but ethnicity was seen as too fundamental to political loyalties to be safely—or fairly—ignored. In this context, what was seen as a relatively uncontentious practice of matching the composition of legislative assemblies to the overall levels of party political support was preferred over a more dangerous and troubling alternative that would give ethnic politics too much power. The distribution of representatives would then, it was hoped, roughly reflect the coun-

---

[31] G. Maré, *Brothers Born of Warrior Blood: Politics and Ethnicity in South Africa* (Johannesburg, 1992), 108.

try's ethnic composition, but it would do this without giving explicit legitimacy to ethnic and racial divisions.

Interestingly enough, Hanna Pitkin made no particular distinction between these two kinds of proportionality when she explored what she saw as the limits to 'mirror' or 'descriptive' representation. In her analysis, descriptive representation is something that aims to capture, in some pictorial way, the nature of the nation or of public opinion, and it is this underlying obsession with composition that interests her rather than the kind of painting people might choose. In most of her discussion, she elides the mapping of opinion with the mapping of people, not really distinguishing between a representative sample that might more adequately capture the range of ideas, the range of interests, or the range of socially significant groups. Thus, she moves from a general commentary on descriptive representation as seeking to 'secure in the government a "reflex" of the opinion of the entire electorate',[32] to a supposed illustration of this in Sidney and Beatrice Webb's critique of the composition of the House of Lords. But the Webbs were talking about class and gender composition—'absolutely no members of the manual working class; none of the great class of shopkeepers, clerks and teachers; none of the half of all the citizens who are of the female sex'[33]—and it begs some rather important questions to treat class and gender composition as just a proxy for opinion and ideas. Arguments for the proportional representation of ideas (or, more modestly, of the distribution of party political support) are not the same as arguments for the proportional representation of workers or women. The former, indeed, could be said to undermine any additional importance attached to the latter.

When John Stuart Mill lent his weight to the electoral reforms proposed by Thomas Hare,[34] he defended Hare's system of proportional representation as something that would raise the intellectual calibre of parliamentary representatives (this was always one of Mill's concerns), while simultaneously enabling voters to choose representatives who really shared their own interests and views. Hare's system treated the entire country as if it were a single

---

[32] Pitkin, *The Concept of Representation*, 61.   [33] Ibid. 61.
[34] J. S. Mill, 'Representative Government', reprinted in J. S. Mill, *Three Essays* (Oxford, 1975); T. Hare, *Treatise on the Election of Representatives* (London, 1859).

constituency, and required voters to rank candidates in order of preference, regardless of the area in which they lived. All these preferences then accumulated towards the final outcome, and any
candidate who reached the requisite number, no matter how dispersed his support, would be duly elected. This system of 'personal
representation' operated almost independently of party labels, and
presumed a far more intimate knowledge of each candidate's virtues
and opinions than we can aspire to in conditions of mass democracy,
but it did in principle offer a way through the false packaging of
political opinion. Minority interests and concerns would have far
more room for manœuvre than under the sway of a few major parties, and would be freed from the constraints of geographical districts in which they might be just a tiny minority. Such a system of
proportional representation might not significantly alter the gender
or racial composition of the final assembly, but it would certainly
allow for more sustained representation of currently excluded perspectives and concerns.

Subsequent developments have adapted these principles to the
later practices of party politics, generating such variants as the party
list system, which is widely used across northern Europe, or the
additional member system, which operates in contemporary
Germany. What characterizes these diverse mechanisms is a greater
attention to the *overall* level of electoral support for each of the competing parties, and a greater emphasis on matching this to the final
makeup of the legislative assembly. This may indeed satisfy those
aspects of the politics of presence that are about the false packaging
of political views, but it leaves untouched those other aspects which
revolve around the symbolic element in political representation, the
importance of ensuring more vigorous advocacy for hitherto
excluded groups, and the way that presence can transform the nature
and content of the political agenda. Minority concerns can perhaps
expect a better hearing inside a proportionally constituted legislative
assembly, but any group that has a history of political exclusion will
still face problems in transforming the political agenda—and any
group that is in a numerical minority will still have trouble getting its
preferred policies in place.

In his critique of proportional representation electoral systems,
Charles Beitz argues that there is not a great difference between having the full range of current opinion reflected inside the legislature,

and having it reflected at an earlier stage in internal party debate.[35] Minority groups and opinions will still make their preferences felt even in non-proportional systems: they just do it at an earlier moment, when they argue about party programmes or the choice of party candidates. Systems of proportional representation may be said to encourage a wider range of ideologically distinct political parties, each of which can win enough support to get representatives into the legislative assembly. In contrast to this, the single-member, first-past-the-post, system is more likely to generate a smallish number of viable parties, each of which will probably end up as a 'broad church' coalition that incorporates a variety of political views. What exactly is at stake in preferring one of these over the other? We might be ideological purists, who disdain the muddle and compromise that takes place in broad church parties. Or we might be guardians of political stability, whose worst nightmare is an unstable proliferation of minority parties and who cannot bear political extremes. But the choice hardly seems to come down to high-minded issues of political equality, and it is not really clear that one is more 'fair' than the other. Beitz puts this in particularly strong terms: '[A]lthough it is true that proportional representation achieves one kind of equality that will not normally obtain in district systems, it is a kind of equality in which there is no general reason to take an interest.'[36]

Beitz's comment reflects his more general argument against deducing political institutions and practices from abstract principles of equality or fairness, but it also suggests some of the limits to what can be expected from establishing proportionality according to political ideas. The arguments for political presence have moved in close association with the arguments for electoral systems based on proportional representation: women, for example, have viewed such systems as considerably more favourable to the achievement of gender parity; while recent contributions to the politics of minority representation in the USA have developed a strong case for adopting proportional representation rather than district systems.[37] But when part of the project of the politics of presence is to achieve the inclusion of previously excluded groups, establishing a proportionate representation of existing preferences will never be enough of an answer. This kind of proportionality leaves to one side all those

---

[35] Beitz, *Political Equality*.
[36] Ibid. 140.
[37] See Lani Guinier's arguments, which I discuss more fully in Ch. 4.

unresolved questions about the status of existing preferences; it also sidesteps all those legitimate queries about whether ideas can be separated from presence. We can no longer pretend that the full range of ideas and preferences and alternatives has been adequately represented when those charged with the job of representation are all white or all male or all middle-class; or that democracies have completed their task of political equality when they free up the market in political ideas. The overly cerebral understanding of difference has not engaged sufficiently with the problems of political exclusion, and achieving the proportional representation of the citizens' ideas goes only part of the way towards tackling these problems.

VII

The argument so far establishes the limits of existing procedures of representation, the validity of pursuing some additional or complementary element, and the importance of political presence in preference and policy formation. What it has not yet satisfactorily established is that shared experience can figure as an appropriate, additional, guarantee. A pure politics of ideas may be inadequate, but any simple reversal of this in favour of a politics of shared experience would be equally—if not more—unsatisfactory.

Consider the following very stark assertion, which was the basis on which a group of Frenchwomen laid claim to a place in the Estates General in 1789:

Just as a nobleman cannot represent a plebeian and the latter cannot represent a nobleman, so a man, no matter how honest he may be, cannot represent a woman. Between the representatives and the represented there must be an absolute identity of interests.[38]

Shared experience here took precedence over shared ideas: no amount of thought or sympathy, no matter how careful or honest, could jump the barriers of experience. And conversely, it seems, experience was enough of a guarantee: the adequacy of the representation depended on the degree to which that experience was shared. Yet, faced with that confident assertion of an 'absolute identity of interests', most contemporary theorists would shy away from the

---

[38] Cited by S. Vegetti Finzi, 'Female Identity between Sexuality and Maternity', in Bock and James, *Beyond Equality and Difference* , 128.

suggestion of an essential female or authentic black subject that could be represented by any of its kind. We do not see political views as following in some automatic way from the bare facts of experience, and, apart from anything else, we would question which particular experience was supposed to be shared—being a woman? living in the town rather than the country? being born second in a family of seven? being brought up in a particular class? Most people will accept that experience has a formative influence on political beliefs (otherwise there would be no purchasers of political biographies); and some may go one step further and say that past experience sets a definite limit to the shape of future beliefs. But the notion that shared experience *guarantees* shared beliefs or goals has neither theoretical nor empirical plausibility. It does scant justice to what is a multiplicity of identities and experiences, and it seriously underplays the capacity for reflection and transformation.

One way of thinking of this is in terms of the asymmetry between exposing the problems of exclusion and identifying the difference that inclusion brings about. If there were no significant variations in power or experience, we could expect our political representatives to be randomly distributed across all the differences of gender or ethnicity or race. The fact that they are not indicates that some obstacle stands in the way. If the obstacle is deliberate discrimination, it goes without saying that those who currently monopolize positions of power cannot stand in for those they have excluded. And even if the obstacles prove more structural (as in the different locations men and women occupy in the sexual division of labour), it seems equally inappropriate to rely on one group standing in for the other. These locations will generate significantly different experiences, and, unless the range is reflected in the decision-making assemblies, decisions will express the preoccupations of those already there. With the best will in the world (and all too often we cannot rely on this), people are not good at imagining themselves in somebody else's shoes. We may get better at such acts of imaginative transcendence when our prejudices have been more forcefully exposed, but this happens only when the 'other' has been well represented.

There is an asymmetry, however, between what alerts us to a problem and what counts as a satisfactory solution. I can think of no explanation for women's continuing (if now more patchy) exclusion from national legislatures that does not refer to intentional or structural male power. But the reversal of this will not guarantee that women's needs or interests are then fully and fairly represented. Indeed, in the absence of mechanisms to establish lines of accountability, it is hard to know what I could mean by this phrase. I could argue some fundamental unity between women, some essential set of experiences and interests that can be represented by any interchangeable combination of women. But if I prefer to keep off this terrain, in what sense are women represented by women? The exclusion of women proves that something peculiar is going on. Their subsequent inclusion does not guarantee a solution.

Iris Young gives one possible answer to this conundrum in her argument for specifically *group* representation, which would then depend on a range of enabling conditions that allow the members of the group to formulate their 'group' point of view. This lifts the argument off its uncomfortably essentialist grounding in shared experience or shared identity, for, instead of presuming some innate unity of interests (any woman can speak for all women, or any black person for black people as a whole), Young looks to the political context in which groups can develop their specific concerns. She argues for public funding to facilitate group organization: resources that would help provide means of communication, places to get together, opportunities for meeting and deciding group goals. The people representing the group would then be able to refer back to this process of collective engagement. They would be speaking for their caucus, organization, or group, and they would be conveying the results of what might have been a very contested internal debate.

Young's notion of group representation avoids most of the pitfalls in appealing to shared experience as an automatic guarantee. It makes no claims to essential unities or characteristics; it recognizes the potential diversity and disagreement within any social group; and it provides some basis for the accountability of representatives to those they might claim to represent. But the kind of participatory involvement Young envisages as establishing the priorities and concerns of each group is not yet a serious option at national level; it works best in the context of additional group representation in the process of policy formation. It is perfectly conceivable for the women members of a trade union or professional association to meet together as a caucus and determine their own policy commitments and concerns— though even here, those who involve themselves will be a minority and not fully 'representative' of the women members as a whole. It is virtually impossible, by contrast, to imagine all the women in a country, a constituency, even a neighbourhood, getting together to work out 'their' concerns. This sets far too high a threshold for participation; short of major changes in political culture and practice, it could hardly generate a 'representative' group.

The legitimacy of group representation depends on some mechanism for establishing what the group in question wants or thinks or needs, and there are only two serious candidates for this. One is the implausible essentialism that sees shared experience as enough of a guarantee of shared belief; the other is the organization of some sufficiently representative segment to establish group opinions and goals. If the first is implausible and the second unlikely, then what is at issue in demands for the equal or proportionate presence of members of particular social groups is not strictly 'group representation'. It is more a question of challenging existing exclusions, and opening up opportunities for different issues or concerns to be developed. If it is guarantees that we want, then some form of 'typical' or 'descriptive' representation is hardly the ideal avenue—or, more precisely, it only becomes such when we pursue an unattractively essentialist line.

This is the point at which some readers will throw up their hands in disbelief, for, in declining the support of essential group interest or identity, I may be thought to be abandoning the only legitimate basis for equal or proportionate presence. Representation as currently organized may well be a muddle; it may well be failing to give expression to a wide range of existing and possible preferences; it may well reinforce the dominance of particular social groups. But if the proposed changes in the composition of representative assemblies have no secure grounding in the 'guarantees' of group experience, what is the basis on which these new representatives represent anyone other than themselves?

The question arises with particular intensity in the politics around women's representation, for feminists have been much exercised over matters of essentialism, and most have explicitly repudiated an essential identity of woman. Exceptions can always be found, and many who reject the label still find themselves charged as essentialists by others. But the dominant discourse in contemporary feminism stresses differences *between* women almost as strenuously as differences between women and men. What then is at stake in arguing for a larger contingent of women in elected representative assemblies? What do such women represent if not an essential female interest or identity?

Of the three worries outlined in Chapter 1 (the fear of balkanization, the anxieties over establishing accountability, and the risk of strengthening even further the narrow politics of interest-based groups), it is the second that most concerns me in the next chapter on the political representation of women. Fears of balkanization are largely in abeyance when it comes to women; most women live in households alongside men, and even those who have pursued a more separatist politics and life-style still have to reach accommodation with men in their daily lives and their field of work. The fear of encouraging a more partial interest group politics is somewhat stronger, but this is moderated by feminist insistence on a multiplicity of interests, as well as by the strong tendency within feminism to attack the sordid politics of faction and interest. The question of accountability then emerges as the pre-eminent concern in the following chapter, which examines the four most common arguments for enhancing women's political presence, and the gaps that have to be filled in around the nature of representation and accountability. The calls for gender parity cannot be adequately theorized in terms of representing pre-agreed policies and goals; if the policies were laid out in detail, it would be a matter of less moment whether those implementing them were women or men. The case for gender parity rests heavily on outcomes as yet unknown, and this implies considerably more autonomy for the representatives than has been allowed in the radical tradition. This is, I argue, an inevitable consequence of the politics of presence, for, in challenging the standard exclusions practised in current conventions of party politics, it also distances itself from a politics of binding mandates. This is not to say that accountability drops out of the picture. But accountability is best understood in relation to the politics of ideas—which is one of the reasons, of course, for needing both ideas and presence.

CHAPTER 3

Quotas for women

Though the overall statistics on women in politics continue to tell their dreary tale of under-representation, this under-representation is now widely regarded as a problem, and a significant number of political parties have adopted measures to raise the proportion of women elected. That the issue is even discussed marks a significant change. Even more remarkable is that growing support for a variety of *enabling* devices (day-schools, for example, to encourage potential women candidates) now combines with some minority backing for measures that guarantee parity between women and men. Parties in the Nordic countries took the lead in this, introducing gender quotas for the selection of parliamentary candidates from the mid-1970s onwards, but a quick survey across the globe throws up a number of parallel developments.

When the African National Congress contested its first democratic election in South Africa, it operated a quota for women in selecting the candidates for seats. Recent developments in Indian local government have applied a quota system for people from scheduled castes (this is already practised in employment and education) to elected positions at the village, block, and district level; the Panchayati Acts additionally require that one-third of the seats be reserved for women. Five years ago, the British Labour Party adopted a 50 per cent target for the number of women elected, to be achieved within three general elections. At its annual conference in 1993, it decided to establish all-women short lists for candidate selection in half the 'target' marginals and half the seats where sitting members will retire; since local parties have overall control of their

selection process, it hoped to achieve this through amicable agreement.[1]

The bitter hostility such developments can arouse warns against
easy optimism, but even the bitterness testifies to a sea-change in
political attitudes. Positive action to increase the proportion of
women elected is now on the political agenda. It has become one of
the issues on which politicians disagree.

In some ways, indeed, this is an area in which those engaged in the
practice of politics have edged ahead of those engaged in its theory.
Gatherings of party politicians are significantly more likely to admit
the problem of women's under-representation than gatherings of
political scientists; for, while the former remain deeply divided over
the particular measures they will support, most can manage at least a
lukewarm expression of 'regret' that so few women are elected. The
pressures of party competition weigh heavily on their shoulders. In
an era of increased voter volatility, they cannot afford to disparage
issues that competitors might turn to electoral advantage. Hence the
cumulative effect noted in Norwegian politics, where the Socialist
Left Party first adopted gender quotas in the 1970s, to be followed
in the 1980s by similar initiatives from the Labour and Centre
Parties, and by substantial increases in the number of women
selected by the Conservative Party as well.[2] Hence the impact of the
German Green Party, which decided to alternate women and men on
its list for the 1986 election; the threat of this small—but at the time
rapidly growing—party contributed to the Christian Democrats'
adoption of a voluntary quota, and to the Social Democrats' conver-
sion to a formal one.[3] Hence the otherwise surprising consensus that
has emerged among Britain's major political parties—at central
office level if not yet in local constituencies—in favour of selecting a
higher proportion of women candidates.[4] None of this would have

---

[1] This device reflects the contraints of the British electoral system, which operates with single-member constituencies and first-past-the-post election, and is not
then amenable to the more normal quota procedures.

[2] H. Skjeie, 'The Rhetoric of Difference: On Women's Inclusion into Political
Elites', *Politics and Society*, 19/2 (1991).

[3] J. Chapman, *Politics, Feminism, and the Reformation of Gender* (London,
1993), ch. 9.

[4] J. Lovenduski and P. Norris, 'Selecting Women Candidates: Obstacles to the
Feminisation of the House of Commons', *European Journal of Political Research*,
17 (1989).

happened without vigorous campaigning inside the political parties, but the campaigns have proved particularly effective where parties were already worried about their electoral appeal.

The results are not as yet striking, and outside the Nordic countries political élites continue to be resolutely male: a solid phalanx of dull-suited men, with only the occasional splash of female colour. A comparative survey from 1990 showed the proportion of women in legislative assemblies reaching 38 per cent in Sweden, 34.4 per cent in Norway, 33.5 per cent in Finland, 30.7 per cent in Denmark; then dropping to 21.3 per cent in the Netherlands, 15.4 per cent in Germany, 8.5 per cent in Belgium, 6.3 per cent in the UK, and a mere 5.8 per cent in France.[5] Subsequent elections have brought further modification (the Netherlands has now reached Nordic proportions, while the UK figure jumped to over 9 per cent at the following general election), but the prospects for continuing improvement almost certainly depend on the willingness of political parties to make sex an additional criterion in choosing their candidates. Background changes in society have their effect, and the marked increase in women's labour market participation, combined with the equalization of educational qualifications between the sexes, is likely to feed through gradually into a greater number of women elected. But any more rapid improvement depends on deliberate choice. It is frequently noted that those countries that have adopted multi-member rather than single-member electoral constituencies offer more favourable conditions for women politicians, for when parties are choosing a slate of candidates it looks more obviously indefensible if all of these turn out to be men.[6] The most dramatic changes, however, have occurred where parties are pressured into positive action, setting a minimum target for the number of women elected, or, as in the common Nordic alternative, requiring a 40 per cent minimum for either sex.

Critics of gender parity[7] have tended to home in on what is really

[5] S. McRae, 'Women at the Top: The Case of British National Politics', *Parliamentary Affairs*, 43/3 (1990).

[6] P. Norris, 'Women's Legislative Participation in Western Europe', in S. Bashevkin (ed.), *Women and Politics in Western Europe* (London, 1985).

[7] I use the term 'parity' to indicate a rough equality between the proportion of women and men elected. My use of this term should not be confused with the arguments that have recently surfaced within the Council of Europe for so-called parity democracy. See J. Outshoorn, 'Parity Democracy: A Critical Look at a "New"

a second-order question. Taking it almost as given that the current under-representation of women in elected assemblies is a problem, they focus on what they perceive as the unacceptable solution of positive action. There is a surprising degree of consensus that women *are* under-represented, and few critics have bothered to contest this point. More remarkably still, critics rarely dwell on the essentialist presumptions of 'a' women's perspective, or the dangerous potential for women politicians pressing only narrowly sectional concerns. It is as if there are just too many women for them to be considered as a unified or sectional group, and too obviously spread across every social dimension and every conceivable political persuasion. So, while concerns about social divisiveness and sectional narrowing are part of the standard fare in arguments against other forms of group-based representation, opponents of gender quotas are most likely to take their stand on a general critique of affirmative action, on the paucity of 'experienced' women, and the risk that the overall calibre of politicians will fall.

The argument then becomes a subset of more general debates, focusing on supposed tensions between selection by gender and selection by merit. Those opposed to gender quotas or other such affirmative actions typically insist on the dangers of abandoning meritocratic principles; and they warn the aspiring politicians of the derision that will pursue them if they reach their positions through their gender alone.

Quotas are patronising and self-defeating. Appointing or selecting women on grounds other than ability will rebound, not just on those individuals but on women generally. To say it is merely wiping out a disadvantage is disingenuous. Women will be making progress by denying men an equal chance to compete. How can any woman politician claim to be taken seriously in such circumstances? An unfairness will have been replaced by a deliberate rigging of the rules.[8]

The really reactionary mentality belongs to those who argue that women must be cosseted and promoted by virtue of their sex in a way that men are not.[9]

Strategy', paper prepared for workshop on 'Citizenship and Plurality', European Consortium for Political Research, Leiden, 1993.

[8] M. Phillips, 'Hello to the Gender Gerrymander', *Observer* (3 October 1993).
[9] Editorial, *London Evening Standard* (24 June 1993).

Such arguments lend themselves to a series of empirical contestations, some of which have explored the availability of qualified women, while others query the startling presumption that existing incumbents were chosen on merit. (This last point is nicely summed up in a widely repeated comment that we'll know we have genuine equality when the country is run by incompetent women.) One of the points raised in the wider literature is that, even in the most seemingly meritocratic of systems—the selection of students for academic courses or the appointment of academics to university jobs—there is normally a cluster of vaguer characteristics which can override the stricter numerical hierarchy of grades or publications or degrees.[10] The implication is that selection by 'merit' and selection by ethnicity or gender are not such poles apart, for there is no process of admission or appointment that operates by a single quantifiable scale, and the numbers are always moderated by additional criteria. These more qualitative criteria ('personality', 'character', whether the candidates will 'fit in') often favour those who are most like the people conducting the interview: more starkly, they often favour the men. The point applies *a fortiori* to the process of selecting candidates for political office, where no one really knows what the qualifications should be.

A related point frequently raised in the general literature is that justifiable measures for remedying social disadvantage can come into conflict with what seem equally justifiable claims by individuals who would have got on the course or into the position if they had been around just ten years earlier. Such individuals then seem to be paying unfairly for something that was hardly their personal fault, and even those most committed to affirmative action will sometimes argue a moral case for compensating those who seem singled out to pay what should really be regarded as a social debt.[11] Whatever conclusion we may reach on this, it is a problem that has less obvious application in the political realm. When Abigail Thernstrom wrote her indictment of what she saw as racial gerrymandering in the USA, she noted how extraordinary it was that, in an era marked by sharp challenges to affirmative action in the fields of education and employment, no one seemed particularly bothered by its equally

[10] See P. Green, *The Pursuit of Inequality* (New York, 1981), especially ch. 6.

[11] This argument is comprehensively discussed in G. Ezorsky, *Racism and Justice: The Case for Affirmative Action* (Ithaca, NY, 1991), especially ch. 4.

extensive application in the field of political representation.[12] The explanation for this lies in our very different relationship to electoral office, which we rarely conceive as a matter of individual rights. The most ardent defender of an individual's 'right' to a particular course or a particular position rarely talks of the individual's 'right' to be elected to parliament: outside the great political dynasties, few people think of political office in these terms.

These have been the issues most likely to arise in popular or media discussion, but from my perspective they remain mere skirmishing around the edges. The emphasis is entirely on the legitimacy of particular measures: how is one to justify quotas, guarantees, positive action, what its critics regard as 'reverse discrimination'? The arguments then parallel and reproduce those applied to the use of gender quotas in education or employment, with little sense of what makes political representation different from either of these. This elision obscures more fundamental issues of representation, and this is the first point I want to stress. The argument for gender parity in politics can proceed perfectly happily on the basis of correcting a previous injustice, but where this treats being an elected representative as much the same sort of thing as being a doctor or lawyer or engineer, it does not grapple adequately with what we mean by representation. It may be that this limitation is part of the appeal: that arguing for more women in politics as if this were simply an extension of more women in medicine or more women in law is what makes the case so effective. But what concerns me here is not so much the pragmatic choices over which kind of argument to employ. I want to address the theoretical basis of the arguments, and what they imply about representation.

I

Arguments for raising the proportion of women elected have fallen broadly into four groups. There are those that dwell on the role model successful women politicians offer; those that appeal to principles of justice between the sexes; those that identify particular interests of women that would be otherwise overlooked; and those that stress women's different relationship to politics and the way

[12] A. M. Thernstrom, *Whose Votes Count? Affirmative Action and Minority Voting Rights* (Cambridge, Mass., 1987), 9.

their presence will enhance the quality of political life. The least interesting of these, from my point of view, is the role model. When more women candidates are elected, their example is said to raise women's self-esteem, encourage others to follow in their footsteps, and dislodge deep-rooted assumptions about what is appropriate to women and men. I leave this to one side, for I see it as an argument that has no particular purchase on politics *per se*. Positive role models are certainly beneficial, but I want to address those arguments that engage more directly with democracy.

The most immediately compelling of the remaining arguments is that which presents gender parity as a straightforward matter of justice: that it is patently and grotesquely unfair for men to monopolize representation. If there were no obstacles operating to keep certain groups of people out of political life, we would expect positions of political influence to be randomly distributed between the sexes. There might be some minor and innocent deviations, but any more distorted distribution is evidence of intentional or structural discrimination. In such contexts (that is, most contexts) women are being denied rights and opportunities that are currently available to men. There is a prima facie case for action.

There are two things to be said about this. One is that it relies on a strong position on the current sexual division of labour as inequitable and 'unnatural'. Consider the parallel under-representation of the very young and very old in politics. Most people will accept this as part of a normal and natural life-cycle, in which the young have no time for conventional politics, and the old have already contributed their share; and since each in principle has a chance in the middle years of life, this under-representation does not strike us as particularly unfair. The consequent 'exclusion' of certain views or experiences may be said to pose a problem; but, however much people worry about this, they rarely argue for proportionate representation for the over-70s and the under-25s.[13] The situation of women looks more obviously unfair, in that women will be under-represented throughout their entire lives, but anyone wedded to the current division of labour can treat it as a parallel case. A woman's life-cycle typically includes a lengthy period of caring for children,

[13] There *are* parties that operate quotas for youth (usually defined as under 30), but no one, to my knowledge, argues that voters aged between 18 and 25 should have a proportionate representation in parliament.

and another lengthy period of caring for parents as they grow old. It is hardly surprising, then, that fewer women come forward as candidates, or that so few women are elected. Here, too, there may be an under-representation of particular experiences and concerns, but, since this arises quite 'naturally' from particular life-cycles, it is not at odds with equality or justice.

I do not find the parallel convincing, but my reasons lie in a feminist analysis of the sexual division of labour as 'unnatural' and unjust. The general argument from equal rights or opportunities translates into a specific case for gender parity in politics only when it is combined with some such analysis; failing this, it engages merely with the more overt forms of discrimination that exclude particular aspirants from political office. Justice requires us to eliminate discrimination (this is already implied in the notion of justice), but the argument for women's equal representation in politics depends on that further ingredient which establishes structural discrimination. Feminists will have no difficulty adding this, and the first point then reinforces the general argument already developed in Chapter 2. The case for the proportionate representation of women and men is not something we can deduce from an impossibly abstract equation of fair representation with proportional representation, as if each and every characteristic can be mapped out in the legislative assemblies. Nor is it automatically mandated by the discovery that there are fewer women in politics than men. Something else has to be added before we can move from a description of women's under-representation to an analysis of its injustice.

The second point is more intrinsically problematic, and relates to the status of representation as a political act. If we treat the under-representation of women in politics as akin to their under-representation in management or the professions, we seem to treat being a politician as on a continuum with all those other careers that should be opened up equally to women. In each case, there is disturbing evidence of sexual inequality; in each case, there should be positive action for change. The argument appeals to our sense of justice, but it does so at the expense of an equally strong feeling that being a politician is not just another kind of job. 'Career politician' is still (and surely rightly) a term of abuse; however accurately it may describe people's activities in politics, it does not capture our political ideals. If political office *has* been reduced to yet another

favourable and privileged position, then there is a clear argument
from justice for making such office equally available to women.
Most democrats, however, will want to resist pressures to regard
political office in this way. So, while men have no 'right' to monopolize political office, there is something rather unsatisfying in basing women's claim to political equality on an equal right to an
interesting job.

Reformulating the equal right to political office as an equal right to
participate in politics makes it sound much better, but does not otherwise help. A rough equality in political participation has entered
firmly enough into the understanding (if not yet the practice) of political equality for us to see an imbalance between the sexes as a legitimate
cause for concern. Extending this, however, to the sphere of representation simply asserts what has to be established: that representation is
just another aspect of participation, to be judged by identical criteria.
The under-representation of women in elected assemblies is not
simply analogous to their under-representation in the membership of
political parties or the attendance at political meetings; for, while we
can quite legitimately talk of an equal 'right' to political participation,
we cannot so readily talk of an equal 'right' to be elected to political
office. As has already been noted, the deduction from the one to the
other lays itself open to irritated complaints of missing what is new
about representation.

What we can more usefully do is turn the argument around, and
ask by what 'natural' superiority of talent or experience men could
claim a right to dominate assemblies? The burden of proof then
shifts to the men, who would have to establish either some genetic
distinction which makes them better at understanding problems and
taking decisions, or some more socially derived advantage which
enhances their political skills. Neither of these looks particularly
persuasive; the first has never been successfully established, and the
second is no justification if it depends on structures of discrimination. There is no argument from justice that can defend the current
state of affairs; and in this more negative sense, there *is* an argument
from justice for parity between women and men. The case then
approximates that more general argument about symbolic representation, stressing the social significance that attaches to the composition
of political élites, and the way that exclusion from these reinforces
wider assumptions about the inferiority of particular groups. But

there is a troubling sense in which this still overlooks what is peculiar to representation as a political act. When democracy has been
widely understood as a matter of representing particular policies or
programmes or ideas, this leaves a question mark over why the sex
of the representatives should matter.

II

An alternative way of arguing for gender parity is in terms of the
interests that would be otherwise discounted. This is an argument
from political realism. In the heterogeneous societies contained by
the modern nation-state, there is no transparently obvious 'public
interest', but rather a multiplicity of different and potentially
conflicting interests which must be acknowledged and held in check.
Our political representatives are only human, and as such they cannot pretend to any greater generosity of spirit than those who elected
them to office. There may be altruists among them, but it would be
unwise to rely on this in framing our constitutional arrangements.
Failing Plato's solution to the intrusion of private interest (a class of
Guardians with no property or family of their own), we must look
to other ways of limiting tyrannical tendencies, and most of these
will involve giving all interests their legitimate voice.

This, in essence, was James Mill's case for representative government and an extended franchise, though he notoriously combined
this with the argument that women could 'be struck off without
inconvenience' from the list of potential claimants, because they had
no interests not already included in those of their fathers or husbands. (He also thought we could strike off 'young' men under forty
years of age.) Part of the argument for increasing women's political
representation is a feminist rewrite and extension of this. Women
occupy a distinct position within society: they are typically concentrated, for example, in lower paid jobs; and they carry the primary
responsibility for the unpaid work of caring for others. There are
particular needs, interests, and concerns that arise from women's
experience, and these will be inadequately addressed in a politics that
is dominated by men. Equal rights to a vote have not proved strong
enough to deal with this problem; there must also be equality among
those elected to office.

One point made by Will Kymlicka is that this argument may not be enough to justify parity of presence. In a recent discussion of demands for group representation in Canada, he makes a useful distinction between arguments for equal or proportionate presence (where the number of women or Aboriginal peoples or francophone Canadians in any legislative assembly would correspond to their proportion in the citizenry as a whole), and the case for a threshold presence (where the numbers would reach the requisite level that ensured each group's concerns were adequately addressed).[14] When the group in question is a numerically small minority, the threshold might prove larger than their proportion in the population as a whole; when the group composes half the population, the threshold might be considerably lower. On this basis, there could be an argument for greater than proportionate representation of Aboriginal peoples, for example, but less than proportionate representation of women—not that women would be formally restricted to 25 per cent or 30 per cent of the seats, but that they might not require any more than this in order to change the political agenda. It is the argument from justice that most readily translates into strict notions of equality; the argument from women's interests need not deliver such strong results.

The above is a qualification rather than a counter-argument, and in principle it still confirms the legitimacy of political presence. A potentially more damaging argument comes from those who query whether women do have a distinct and separate interest, and whether 'women' is a sufficiently unified category to generate an interest of its own. If women's interests differed systematically from men's (or if women always thought differently on political issues), then the disproportionate number of men in politics would seem self-evidently wrong. The concerns of one group would get minimal consideration; the concerns of another would have excessive weight. But where is the evidence for this claim? Does not the notion of a distinct 'women's interest' just dissolve upon closer attention?

The idea that women have at least some interests distinct from and even in conflict with men's is, I think, relatively straightforward. Women have distinct interests in relation to child-bearing (for any foreseeable future, an exclusively female affair); and as society is currently constituted they also have particular interests arising from

[14] W. Kymlicka, *Multicultural Citizenship: A Liberal Theory of Minority Rights* (Oxford, 1995), ch. 7.

their exposure to sexual harassment and violence, their unequal position in the division of paid and unpaid labour, and their exclusion
from most arenas of economic or political power.[15] But all this may
still be said to fall short of establishing a set of interests shared by all
women. If interests are understood in terms of what women express
as their priorities and goals, there is considerable disagreement
among women; and, while attitude surveys frequently expose a 'gender gap' between women and men, the more striking development
over recent decades has been the convergence in the voting behaviour of women and men. There may be more mileage in notions of a
distinct woman's interest if this is understood in terms of some
underlying but as yet unnoticed 'reality', but this edges uncomfortably close to notions of 'false consciousness', which most feminists
would prefer to avoid. Indeed, the presumption of a clearly demarcated woman's interest which holds true for all women in all classes
and all countries has been one of the casualties of recent feminist critique, and the exposure of multiple differences between women has
undermined more global understandings of women's interests and
concerns.[16] If there is no clearly agreed woman's interest, can this
really figure as a basis for more women in politics?

There are two things to be said about this. The first is that the variety of women's interests does not refute the claim that interests are
gendered. That some women do not bear children does not make
pregnancy a gender-neutral event; that women disagree so profoundly on abortion does not make its legal availability a matter of
equal concern to both women and men; that women occupy such
different positions in the occupational hierarchy does not mean they
have the same interests as men in their class. The argument from
interest does not depend on establishing a unified interest of all
women: it depends, rather, on establishing a difference between the
interests of women and men.

Some of the interests of women will, of course, overlap with the

---

[15] Since segregation is the fundamental ordering principle of gendered societies,
women can be said to share at least one interest in common: the interest in improved
access. See H. Skjeie, *The Feminization of Power: Norway's Political Experiment
(1986–)* (Oslo, 1988).

[16] See e.g. C. T. Mohanty, 'Feminist Encounters: Locating the Politics of
Experience', in M. Barrett and A. Phillips (eds.), *Destabilizing Theory: Contemporary Feminist Debates* (Cambridge, 1993).

interests of certain groups of men. The fact that women are more likely to depend on public transport, for example, forges a potential alliance with those men who have campaigned for better public transport on social or environmental grounds; and the fact that women are more likely to press the interests of children does not mean that no man would share their concerns. In these instances, it may be said that the election of more female representatives will introduce a new range of issues—but that many of these will be ones that some men will be happy to endorse. In other instances, the differences are more inherently conflictual. Women's claim to equal pay must, logically, imply a relative worsening of male earnings; and outside extraordinary growth conditions, women's claim to equal employment opportunities must reduce some of the openings currently available to men. Women have no monopoly on generosity of spirit, and even in these more conflictual situations they can expect to find a few powerful allies among the men. What they cannot really expect is the degree of vigorous advocacy that people bring to their own concerns.

The second point is more complex, and arises with particular pertinence when a history of political exclusion has made it hard even to articulate group concerns. When Hanna Pitkin explored Edmund Burke's rather odd understanding of representation, she noted that he conceived of interests as a matter of 'objective, impersonal, unattached reality';[17] this then became the basis on which he argued for 'virtual' representation, by people not even chosen by the interested group. Burke certainly thought that all major interests should be duly represented, but the very objectivity of the interests allowed for their representation by people who did not immediately share them. The more fixed the interests, the more definite and easily defined, the less significance seemed to attach to who does the work of representation. So if women's interests had a more objective quality (and were transparently obvious to any intelligent observer) there might be no particular case—beyond what I have already argued about vigorous advocacy—for insisting on representatives who also happen to be women. We might feel that men would be less diligent in pressing women's interests and concerns, that their declared 'sympathy' would always be suspect. But if we all knew what these

[17] H. Pitkin, *The Concept of Representation* (Berkeley, 1967), 168.

interests were, it would be correspondingly easy to tell whether or not they were being adequately pursued.

Interest would then more obviously parallel political ideas or beliefs. It would become something we could detach from particular experience, as we already detach the 'interest' of pensioners, or children, or the long-term unemployed. Each of these (perhaps particularly the example of children) is problematic, but in each of them we can more legitimately claim to know what is in a group's interest. Attention then shifts to more traditional ways of strengthening the weight attached to the interests, perhaps through writing them into party programmes or party commitments. The alternative emphasis on changing the composition of decision-making assemblies is particularly compelling where interests are not so precisely delineated, where the political agenda has been constructed without reference to certain areas of concern, and where much fresh thinking is necessary to work out what best to do. In such contexts there is little to turn to other than the people who carry the interests, and who does the representation then comes to be of equal significance with what political parties they represent.

This argument echoes what was a widely shared experience in the early years of contemporary feminism. The now derided emphasis on consciousness-raising groups offered more than a luxury occasion for some women to get together and moan: the sharing of experience was part of a process in which women freed themselves from a cycle of passivity and self-denial, stretched their sense of what was possible and desirable, and reached different conclusions about what they might want. Those involved in this experience frequently talked of their difficulties in finding a voice, the way that dominant definitions of politics blocked out alternatives, or hegemonic culture controlled what could or could not be said. The emphasis then shifted from an objectively defined set of interests (which just needed more vigorous pursuit) to a more exploratory notion of possibilities so far silenced and ideas one had to struggle to express. And in this later understanding of the processes that generate needs and concerns and ideas, it was far harder to sustain the primacy of ideas over political presence. If the field of politics has already been clearly demarcated, containing within it a comprehensive range of ideas and interests and concerns, it might not so much matter who does the work of representation. But if the range of ideas has been curtailed by orthodoxies that rendered alternatives invisible, there will be no satisfactory solution short of changing the people who represent and develop the ideas.

The more decisive problem with the argument from interests lies in the conditions for accountability to the interested group. Does the election of more women ensure their representation? At an intuitive level, an increase in the number of women elected seems likely to change both the practices and priorities of politics, increasing the attention given to matters of child care, for example, or ensuring that women's poor position in the labour market is more vigorously addressed. This intuition is already partially confirmed by the experience of those countries that have changed the gender composition of their elected assemblies. But what does this mean in terms of political representation? Elections are typically organized by geographical constituencies, which sometimes coincide with concentrations of particular ethnic or religious groups, or concentrations of certain social classes, but which never coincide with concentrations of women or men. Elections typically take place through the medium of political parties, each of which produces candidates who are said to represent that party's policies and programmes and goals. In what sense can we say that the women elected through this process carry an additional responsibility to represent women? In the absence of mechanisms to establish acccountability, the equation of more women with more adequate representation of women's interests looks suspiciously undemocratic. If the interests of women are varied, or not yet fully formed, how do the women elected know what the women who elected them want? By what right do they claim their responsibility to represent women's concerns? The asymmetry between noting a problem of exclusion and identifying the difference that inclusion brings about is particularly pointed here. However plausible it is to say that male-dominated assemblies will not adequately address the needs and interests of women, it cannot be claimed with equal confidence that a more balanced legislature will fill this gap.

III

The third way of formulating the case for gender parity approaches it from almost the opposite direction. It sees the inclusion of women as challenging the dominance of interest group politics, and expects women politicians to introduce a different set of values and concerns. This is something that has had a long history in feminist thinking; for, while women have repeatedly complained that their interests were being ignored by the men, the very same women have often presented their sex as the one that disdains interest and transcends the limits of faction. In the campaign for women's suffrage, for example, it was often suggested that women would bring a more generous morality to the political field; in the recent development of eco-feminism, it is often argued that women have a deeper, because trans-generational, relationship to the needs of the environment.

In some formulations of this, feminists have made a strong distinction between interest and need, arguing that the emphasis on interests treats politics as a matter of brokerage between different groups, and that the equation of politics with the rational calculation of interests is at odds with women's own understanding of their needs and goals.[18] As Irene Diamond and Nancy Hartsock put it, '[t]he reduction of all human emotions to interests, and interests to the rational search for gain reduces the human community to an instrumental, arbitrary, and deeply unstable alliance, one which rests on the private desires of isolated individuals.'[19] Need, by contrast, is thought to appeal to a more basic and common humanity; instead of asserting a stake in political battle, it formulates claims in more obviously moral terms.

This distinction engages directly with that common objection to a politics of presence which views it as increasing the role of interest in politics. When the demand for more women in politics is formulated in terms of interest, this seems to accept a version of politics as a matter of competition between interest groups; it talks the language of defence or protection, and treats politics as a zero-sum game. But when the demand is formulated in terms of need, this potentially raises things to a higher plain. The substitution of needs talk for interests talk may then offer a more radical challenge to the practices

[18] J. Jacquette, 'Power as Ideology: A Feminist Analysis', in J. S. Stiehm (ed.), *Women's Views of the Political World of Men* (New York, 1984).

[19] I. Diamond and N. Hartsock, 'Beyond Interests in Politics: A Comment on Virginia Sapiro's "When are interests interesting?" ' *American Political Science Review*, 75/3 (1981), 719.

of contemporary democracy, querying the very nature of the game as well as the composition of the players.

My own position on this is somewhat agnostic. Interest can sound rather grasping and competitive, but it does at least serve to remind us that there may be conflicts between different groups. Need has more obvious moral resonance, but it originates from a paternalist discourse which lends itself more readily to decisions by experts on behalf of the needy group.[20] My own rather commonsensical solution is to use both terms together. Note, however, that the opposition between need and interest does not substantially alter what is at issue in demands for more women in politics, for need is as contested as interest, and either requires a greater female presence. As Nancy Fraser has argued, the interpretation of needs is itself a matter of political struggle, spanning three crucial moments: the struggle to establish (or deny) the political status of a given need; the struggle for the power to define and interpret the need; and the struggle to secure its satisfaction.[21] At each moment it matters immensely who can claim the authoritative interpretation; and, while much of the battle for this rages across the full terrain of civil society, groups excluded from state agencies or legislative assemblies will have significantly less chance of establishing their own preferred version. Neither needs nor interests can be conceived as transparently obvious, and any fair interpretation of either then implies the presence of the relevant group.

The broader claim made by those who disdain the politics of interest is that increasing the proportion of women elected introduces new kinds of behaviour and values. It is often suggested, for example, that women will be less competitive, more co-operative, more prepared to listen to others; that women bring with them a different, and more generous, scale of values; that women raise the moral tenor of politics. These arguments are always associated with women's role as caring for others, and often more specifically with

[20] This is one of the arguments made by Anna Jonasdottir, who sees needs talk as potentially paternalist, and not sufficiently insistent on the political involvement of those in need; see her 'On the Concept of Interest, Women's Interests, and the Limitation of Interest Theory', in K. B. Jones and A. Jonasdottir, *The Political Interests of Women* (London, 1988).

[21] N. Fraser, 'Struggle Over Needs: Outline of a Socialist–Feminist Critical Theory of Late Capitalist Political Culture', in N. Fraser, *Unruly Practices: Power, Discourse and Gender in Contemporary Social Theory* (Cambridge, 1989).

their role as mothers. Jean Bethke Elshtain, for example, presents a stark picture of contemporary politics as dominated by the most crass individualism and expressed in the most impersonal of languages: a world that begins and ends 'with mobilization of resources, achieving maximum impacts, calculating prudentially, articulating interest group claims, engaging in reward distribution functions'.[22] The relationship between mother and child then appears as a paradigm for a less interest-regarding set of values. Mothers cannot put their own interests first, for they can never forget the vulnerability of the human child. The politics that develops out of this cannot accept the conventional separation of politics from morality, and it offers the most profound and hopeful challenge to the sordid instrumentalism of the modern world.[23]

Elshtain is only moderately (if at all) concerned with measures that might increase the proportion of women elected, for much of her critique of the current relationship between public and private revolves around an analysis of that world of 'formal' male power which has absorbed more and more spheres of social life into its orbit. She sees little to gain in the absorption of women into the same circuit. But her broadly 'maternal feminism'[24] finds many echoes in current explorations of women's role in politics, perhaps most notably in the Nordic tradition which sees women as bearers of a new 'politics of care'. Feminists have challenged the 'misplaced analogy to the marketplace'[25] which is said to weaken both the theory and practice of politics; they have elaborated alternative theories of power which stress power as energy or capacity rather than dominance; and they have suggested that we try out what society would look like if we conceive it from the perspective of mothering rather than that of 'economic man'.[26] Running through all such arguments

---

[22] J. B. Elshtain, *Public Man, Private Woman: Women in Social and Political Thought* (Princeton, 1981), 246.

[23] J. B. Elshtain, 'The Power and Powerlessness of Women', in G. Bock and S. James (eds.), *Beyond Equality and Difference* (London, 1993).

[24] The phrase comes from Sara Ruddick's 'Maternal Thinking', *Feminist Studies*, 6 (1980).

[25] J. Mansbridge, 'Feminism and Democracy', *American Prospect*, 1 (1990), 134.

[26] V. Held, 'Mothering versus Contract', in J. J. Mansbridge (ed.), *Beyond Self-Interest* (Chicago and London, 1990). Held is careful to clarify that she is not proposing the mother–child relationship as the paradigm for all social relations; she follows Michael Walzer in considering that different paradigms will be appropriate in different domains.

is a consistent contrast between women and the politics of self-interest. The kind of changes we can anticipate from women's increased political presence are seen as relating to this.

My problem with such arguments is not that they presume a difference between men and women. As Catherine MacKinnon puts it in a nicely pointed question, 'I mean, can you imagine elevating one half of a population and denigrating the other half and producing a population in which everyone is the same?'[27] We do not have to resort to either mysticism or socio-biology to explain social differences between women and men, and it would be most peculiar if the different responsibilities the sexes carry for caring for others did not translate into different approaches to politics and power. These initial differences may be far outweighed by the common experiences men and women will later share in making their way through political life. I incline to the view that politics is more formative than sex, and that the contrast between those who get involved in politics and those who do not is deeper than any gender difference between those who are elected. But this remains at a more speculative level. The real problem with basing the case for more women in politics on their supposed superiority over men is that this loads too much on women's role as mothers.

As Mary Dietz, in particular, has argued,[28] the characteristics that make a good mother are not necessarily those that make a good citizen, and the generous care women may give to their dependent children is hardly a paradigm for a democratic politics that should be based on equality and mutual respect. Nor is it particularly useful to present women as better or more moral than men. 'Such a premise would posit as a starting point precisely what a democratic attitude must deny—that one group of citizens' voices is generally better, more deserving of attention, more worthy of emulation, more moral, than another's. A feminist democrat cannot give way to this sort of temptation, lest democracy itself lose its meaning, and citizenship its special name.'[29]

[27] C. A. MacKinnon, *Feminism Unmodified: Discourses on Life and Law* (Cambridge, Mass., 1987), 37.

[28] M. Dietz. 'Citizenship with a Feminist Face: The Problem with Maternal Thinking', *Political Theory*, 13/1 (1985); M. Dietz, 'Context Is All: Feminism and Theories of Citizenship', *Daedalus*, 116/4 (1987); N. Fraser, 'The Ethic of Solidarity', *Praxis International* (1986).

[29] Dietz, 'Context Is All', 17–18.

Which is not to say that women will not, or should not, make a difference. In a recent study of Norwegian MPs, Hege Skjeie uncovered a remarkable consensus across the parties and between the sexes that gender does and should make a difference, with a clear majority thinking that gender affects priorities and interests, and that women represent a new 'politics of care'. Translated into areas of policy initiative, this generated a rather predictable list: politicians of both sexes saw women as particularly concerned with policies on welfare, the environment, equality, education, and disarmament, and men as more interested in the economy, industry, energy, national security, and foreign affairs. (Transport was the only area regarded as equally 'male' and 'female—not because transport is intrinsically more gender-neutral, but because it has become important, for different reasons, to both women and men.) Against the background of a strong Norwegian tradition of social representation, which has long assumed that political representatives should 'mirror' differences between town and country and balance territorial concerns,[30] it has been seen as perfectly legitimate and desirable that women politicians should represent different concerns. Indeed, '[a] mandate of "difference" is now attached to women politicians . . . Women have entered politics on a collective mandate, and their performance is judged collectively.'[31]

The precise implications of this remain, however, ambiguous. The widely presumed association between women and a politics of care leaves it open whether women will concentrate on policies to enhance child care provision, thereby to increase women's participation in the labour market, or on policies that will raise the value and prestige of the care work that women do in the home. What resolves this in the Norwegian context is not so much gender as party. Women associated with parties on the left of the political spectrum are more likely to interpret a politics of care in terms of the first set of priorities, while women associated with parties on the right will tend to the second interpretation. In this as in other policy areas, party loyalties are usually decisive, and, though Skjeie notes a number of cases of women forming cross-party alliances on particular

[30] H. Valen, 'Norway: Decentralization and Group Representation', in M. Gallagher and M. Marsh (eds.), *Candidate Selection in Comparative Perspective* (London, 1988).
[31] Skjeie, 'Rhetoric of Difference', 234.

issues, she finds little evidence of women refusing the ultimate priorities of their parties. 'The belief in women's difference could still turn into a mere litany on the importance of difference. Repeated often enough, the statement that "gender matters" may in turn convince the participants that change can in fact be achieved by no other contribution than the mere presence of women.'[32]

IV

This leads directly into the key area of contention, already signalled in my discussion of interest. Either gender does make a difference, in which case it is in tension with accountability through political parties, or it does not make a difference, in which case it can look a rather opportunistic way of enhancing the career prospects of women politicians. Aside from the symbolic importance of political inclusion, and women's equal right to have their chance at a political career (a fair enough argument, but not intrinsically about democracy), we can only believe that the sex of the representatives matters if we think it will change what the representatives do. Yet in saying this, we seem to be undermining accountability through party programmes. We are saying we expect our representatives to do more—or other—than they promised in the election campaign. If we are either surprised or disappointed, for example, by the limited capacity to act on a cross-party basis, this must be because we see an increase in the number of women politicians as challenging the dominance of the party system, or the tradition of voting along party lines. Those who have felt that tight controls of party discipline have worked to discourage serious discussion and debate may be happy enough with this conclusion. But in the absence of alternative mechanisms of consultation or accountability, it does read like a recipe for letting representatives do what *they* choose to do.

Though it is rarely stated in the literature, the argument from women's interests or needs or difference implies that representatives will have considerable autonomy; that they do have currently; and, by implication, that this ought to continue. Women's exclusion from politics is said to matter precisely because politicians do not abide by pre-agreed policies and goals—and feminists have much experience

[32] Ibid. 258.

of this, gained through painful years of watching hard-won commitments to sexual equality drop off the final agenda. When there is a significant under-representation of women at the point of final decision, this can and does have serious consequences, and it is partly in reflection on this that many have shifted attention from the details of policy commitments to the composition of the decision-making group. Past experience tells us that all male or mostly male assemblies have limited capacity for articulating either the interests or needs of women, and that trying to tie them down to pre-agreed programmes has had only limited effect. There is a strong dose of political realism here. Representatives *do* have autonomy, which is why it matters who those representatives are.

This is a fair enough comment on politics as currently practised, and shifting the gender balance of legislatures then seems a sensible enough strategy for the enfeebled democracies of the present day. But one might still ask whether representatives *should* have such autonomy, and whether it would change the importance attached to gender composition if the politicians were more carefully bound by their party's commitments and goals. Consider, in this context, the guidelines that were introduced by the US Democrats in the early 1970s, to make their National Convention (which carries the crucial responsibility of deciding on the presidential candidate) more representative of the party rank and file. Dismay at the seemingly undemocratic nature of the 1968 Convention prompted the formation of a Commission on Party Structure and Delegate Selection, which recommended more extensive participation by party members in the selection of delegates, as well as quota guidelines to increase the proportion of delegates who were female, black, and young. As a result of this, the composition of the 1972 Convention was markedly more 'descriptive' of party members than previous ones had been: 40 per cent of the delegates were women, 15 per cent were black, and 21 per cent were aged 18–30.[33] But the reforms pointed in potentially contradictory directions, for they simultaneously sought to increase rank-and-file participation in the selection of delegates, to bind

[33] This compared with 15% women, 5% black people, and only 4% aged 18–30 at the 1968 National Convention; see J. I. Lengle, 'Participation, Representation, and Democratic Party Reform', in B. Grofman, A. Lijphart, R. B. McKay and H. A. Scarrow (eds.), *Representation and Redistricting Issues* (Lexington, Mass., 1982), 175.

delegates more tightly to the preferences of this rank and file, and to ensure a more descriptive representation according to age, gender, and race. As Austin Ranney (one of the members of the Commission) later noted, the success of the first two initiatives undermined the importance of the third. By 1980 the overwhelming majority of delegates were being chosen in party primaries which bound them to cast their votes for one particular candidate; they became in consequence mere ciphers, who were there to register preferences already expressed. 'If that is the case,' Ranney argues, 'then it really doesn't matter very much who the delegates are.'[34] The more radical the emphasis on accountability, the less significance attaches to who does the work of representation.

Bob Goodin offers one way out of this impasse, which stresses the importance of symbolic representation and the way this relates to people's self-images in politics.[35] Empirical studies of the 1972 National Convention suggest that increasing the proportion of female and black delegates had minimal impact on the kinds of views represented at the convention, and that neither sex nor race made much of a difference. But such investigations may miss the point, which is that 'people's self-images are, at least in part, tied up with politics'.[36] If the pattern of representation gives no recognition to the communal attachments through which people live their lives, then this is felt to be intolerable, even when changing that pattern of representation has no discernible impact on the kinds of policies adopted. Politics is not just about self-interest, but also about self-image: '[b]e they manifestations of silly sentimentality or not, symbolic appeals have a powerful political pull which social scientists cannot ignore.'[37]

Goodin's argument captures much of the popular impetus towards gender parity, for people do recoil from the representation of themselves by such an 'unrepresentative' sample, and do feel that changing this matters even if it subsequently proves to make no further difference. One of the principles associated with legal judgements is that justice must not only be done but be seen to be done.

[34] A. Ranney, 'Comments on Representation within the Political Party System', in B. Grofman, A. Lijphart, R. B. McKay, and H. A. Scarrow (eds.), *Representation and Redistricting Issues*, (Lexington, Mass., 1982), 196.

[35] R. E. Goodin, 'Convention Quotas and Communal Representation', *British Journal of Political Science*, 7/2 (1977).

[36] Ibid. 259.   [37] Ibid.

By the same token, we might well say that representatives must not only be representative but also be seen to be so. It would be foolish to underplay this element, but it would also be misleading to consider it the only thing at issue in demands for political presence. Women *do* think that it will—or should—make a difference when more women are elected as representatives, and this conviction is equally strong in the arguments I address in the following chapter over the representation of minority Americans. Where this is so, it conflicts with alternative strategies for keeping representatives accountable.

This points to a significant area of divergence between current feminist preoccupations and what has long been the main thrust in radical democracy. Radical democrats distrust the wayward autonomy of politicians and the way they concentrate power around them, and they typically work to combat these tendencies by measures that will bind politicians more tightly to their promises, and disperse over-centralized power. Feminists have usually joined forces in support of the second objective: feminism is widely associated with bringing politics closer to home; and women are often intensely involved in local and community affairs. But when feminists insist that the sex of the representatives matters, they are expressing a deeper ambivalence towards the first objective. The politics of binding mandates turns the representatives into glorified messengers: it puts all the emphasis on to the content of the messages, and makes it irrelevant who the messengers are. In contesting the sex of the representatives, feminists are querying this version of democratic accountability.

What makes sense of this are the arguments developed in Chapter 2 about the limits of a system of representation that is premised on packages of supposedly congruent beliefs, combined with arguments that will be developed in Chapter 6 on the role of deliberation in politics. Much more can (and in my view should) be done to keep representatives accountable to the programmes on which they were elected to office, and to bind them more closely to what they professed as their political beliefs. But there is no combination of reforms that can deliver express and prior commitments on every issue that will come to matter, and it is in those spaces where we have to rely on representatives exercising their own judgement that it can most matter who the representatives are. Behind the deceptive simplicity of the arguments for gender parity is this alternative—and more contested—understanding of representation.

The first part of the argument for gender parity in politics derives from principles of justice, and its power is essentially negative: by what possible superiority of talent or experience could men claim a 'right' to monopolize assemblies? There is no convincing answer to this ultimately rhetorical question, and on this more limited ground of equal access to elected office it is easy enough to establish the case. There are all kinds of second-order questions, relating to how legitimate objectives can be best achieved; and all kinds of pragmatic judgements to be made on specific proposals, none of which flows directly from conclusions on overall objectives. But the real problem with the argument from justice is that it remains a subset of more general arguments for equal opportunities and affirmative action, and as such it gives too little weight to the difference between being a representative and being a lawyer or professor. It may be said that changing the composition of elected assemblies plays a particularly important symbolic role, that it involves a more powerful and visible assertion of women's equality with men than changing the composition of management or the professions. But this still confines it to the realm of symbolic representation, without any clear implications as to what futher difference this representation should make.

The argument from either interests or needs, by contrast, anticipates a difference in the kinds of policy decision that will be made, and this more directly challenges existing conditions of representation and accountability. Representation as currently practised rests on what most of the practitioners will admit is pretence: a pretence that the choices offered to the electorate exhaust the full range of possible alternatives; a pretence that party manifestos and programmes wrap up coherent packages of interests and beliefs; a pretence that government is just a matter of implementing the choices the electorate has made. The pretence cedes tremendous power to those individuals who are eventually elected. (Indeed, in the British system of government, which enforces tight voting discipline on backbench MPs, this power is even further concentrated among those who hold ministerial office.) The power of the representatives is not, of course unlimited; if nothing else, they have to tread in wary judgement of how much the electorate will swallow, and in contemporary mass democracies they pay close attention to the messages that arrive daily through opinion polls. But opinion polls register opinion on what is already on the political agenda, and have never proved a particularly effective way of introducing new possibilities and concerns. They cannot give a significant voice to those groups that have been excluded from arenas of power.

Changing the gender composition of elected assemblies is a major, and necessary, challenge to the social arrangements which have systematically placed women in a subordinate position; and whether we conceive of politics as the representation of interest or need (or both), a closer approximation to gender parity is one minimal condition for transforming the political agenda. But changing the gender composition cannot guarantee that women's needs or interests will then be addressed. The only secure guarantees would be those grounded in an essential identity of women, or those arrived at through mechanisms of accountability to women organized as a separate group. The first has neither empirical nor theoretical plausibility; the second is impossible under current electoral arrangements, and perhaps unlikely in any event. So the case for gender parity among our political representatives inevitably operates in a framework of probabilities rather than certainties. It is possible—if highly unlikely—that assemblies composed equally of women and men will behave just like assemblies in which women have a token presence; it is possible—and perhaps very likely—that they will address the interests of certain groups of women while ignoring the claims of others. The proposed change cannot bring with it a certificate of interests addressed or even a guarantee of good intent. In this, as in all areas of politics, there are no definitive guarantees.

Although the importance I have attached to the gender of the representatives conflicts with much of what Hanna Pitkin has argued about the limits of mirror representation, it should be clear from this chapter that I am very much at one with her in seeing representation as a process. Fair representation is not something that can be achieved in one moment, nor is it something that can be guaranteed in advance. Representation depends on the continuing relationship between representatives and the represented, and anyone concerned about the exclusion of women's voices or needs or interests would be ill-advised to shut up shop as soon as half those elected are women. This is already well understood in relation to the politics of ideas; for getting one's preferred party elected to government is usually seen as the beginning rather than the end of the process, and only the most sanguine of voters regards this as settling future policy direction. The warning is even more pointed in relation to the politics of presence, for the shared experience of women as women can only ever figure as a *promise* of shared concerns, and there is no obvious way of establishing strict accountability to women as a group. Changing the gender composition of elected assemblies is largely an enabling condition (a crucially important one, considering what is *dis*abled at present) but it cannot present itself as a guarantee. It is, in some sense, a shot in the dark: far more likely to reach its target than when those shooting are predominantly male, but still open to all kinds of accident.

CHAPTER 4

Race-conscious districting
in the USA

Despite the outrage that continues to attend proposals for gender quotas, measures to increase the proportion of women elected are now sufficiently embedded in the politics of a sufficient number of parties for us to talk of an unstoppable momentum. The speed of change varies considerably from country to country, and much of this variation depends on the degree of commitment to positive action. But even among those most resistant to any system of quotas, the relative under-representation of women is widely regarded as a problem. The very attention devoted to this marks a major success for the politics of presence.

The other major success story comes from the USA, where civil rights litigation has interpreted the 1965 Voting Rights Act to imply the right of minority voters to elect 'the candidates of their choice'. When first introduced, the legislation was concerned primarily with guaranteeing black voters their equal right to vote. This had been blatantly trampled on in much of the deep South, where overtly discriminatory literacy tests (backed up by all kinds of additional requirements for those who successfully negotiated the first stage) had kept black voters off the electoral roll. The legislation established federal control and review over electoral arrangements in the more dicey areas. Section 2 of the Act prohibited the use of electoral practices that could be shown to infringe the right to vote on the basis of race or colour; Section 4 suspended literacy tests and related devices in those states that enfranchised less than half of their voting age population; these states then had to submit future changes in electoral practice to federal scrutiny and approval. The conditions were imposed in six southern states and much of a seventh, and led to a rapid and substantial increase in the numbers of black people registered to vote.

The subsequent evolution of the Act extended it to address the right to cast an equally weighted vote, which increasingly meant the creation of black majority districts (and, later, 'supermajority' districts[1]) from which black voters could elect black representatives. As became clear in a number of contested cases, Southern politicians often sought to minimize the effects of the new electorate by redrawing city boundaries or re-introducing 'at-large' elections.[2] City boundaries were extended to include all-white suburbs, thereby reducing the impact of black inner-city voters; single-member districts in black-majority neighbourhoods were combined with single-member districts in white-majority neighbourhoods to create large multi-member constituencies with an overall white majority.[3] This 'dilution' of the black vote then came to be seen as a new twist in an old story: instead of denying black Americans their right to register as voters, Southern states were denying them the right to cast an 'equally weighted' vote. In a series of legal judgments from the early 1970s onwards, federal courts increasingly ruled against such changes. Voting rights litigation then came to revolve around the formation of single-member electoral districts, with their boundaries drawn so as to coincide with black majorities.

When the Act came up for renewal in 1975, its provisions were

[1] It is frequently argued that blacks or Hispanics need to constitute 60–65% of those within a voting district in order to have a realistic chance of electing 'representatives of their choice'. This is so, it is argued, because of the lower proportion who are of voting age, the lower proportion who register, and the lower proportion who go out to vote. See B. Grofman and L. Handley, 'The Impact of the Voting Rights Act on Black Representation in Southern State Legislatures', *Legislative Studies Quarterly*, 16/1 (1991); and, for a troubled discussion of this, K. Abrams, ' "Raising Politics Up": Minority Political Participation and Section 2 of the Voting Rights Act', *New York University Law Review*, 63/3 (1988).

[2] The multi-member, at-large system dates from turn-of-the-century campaigns against machine politicians who had used single-member district voting to cultivate their local constituencies and buy support through their distribution of political spoils. Samuel Issacharoff argues that, even in this more progressive moment, the introduction of at-large elections was designed to reduce the impact of the white ethnic working-class labour candidates and freed slaves: S. Issacharoff, 'Polarized Voting and the Political Process: The Transformation of Voting Rights Jurisprudence', *Michigan Law Review*, 90/7 (1992).

[3] For examples of such initiatives, see C. Davidson, 'The Voting Rights Act: A Brief History', in B. Grofman and C. Davidson (eds.), *Controversies in Minority Voting: The Voting Rights Act in Perspective* (Washington DC, 1992).

extended to cover states in which there was a significant Hispanic minority, and a similar under-enfranchisement of the voting-age population. This was directed mainly at the Chicanos in the South-West, who had suffered a similar pattern of historical discrimination, including restrictions on their voting rights. At its further renewal in 1982, the Act was amended to permit courts to interpret significant discrepancy between the racial or ethnic composition of the electorate and the racial or ethnic composition of the elected as *de facto* indication that electoral practices might be in violation of the Act. This established what is known as the 'results' test, where discrimination can be established by reference to the effects of electoral practice, without any additional requirement to prove discriminatory intent. The Act has since been extended to apply until 2007.

If we consider the very large number of elected offices in the USA, the results have hardly been spectacular: by the beginning of the 1990s, when black Americans made up 12.4 per cent and Latino Americans 8 per cent of the total population, they occupied only 1.4 per cent and 0.8 per cent respectively of the total elected offices.[4] Measured in absolute terms, the change is more dramatic, with total numbers of black representatives leaping from roughly 500 in the early 1970s to over 6,800 by 1988,[5] and it has been most remarkable of all at the level of city government and state legislature. In 1965, to take just one example, there were only 3 black people elected to the state legislatures in the eleven Southern states of the former Confederacy; by 1985 this had risen to 176, nearly 10 per cent of the total seats.[6] Improvements in Latino representation have been less dramatic, which partly reflects the shorter period over which this has been seriously addressed, and partly the greater heterogeneity of the Latino population.[7] In both cases, however, there has been a

[4] C. Davidson, 'The Voting Rights Act: A Brief History', in Grofman and Davidson, *Controversies in Minority Voting*, 46.

[5] K. Tate, *From Protest to Politics: The New Black Voters in American Elections* (New York, 1993), 1.

[6] Though this still indicates a significant under-representation (black people constitute 20% of the population in these states), it marks major advances in the number of black representatives which would hardly have occurred without the voting rights legislation. See Grofman and Handley, 'Impact of the Voting Rights Act', 112; and similar arguments in many of the essays in Grofman and Davidson, *Controversies in Minority Voting*.

[7] There is some evidence that the electoral change that most promotes the election of black representatives (the shift, that is, from at-large to single-member

significant and substantial change in the composition of political élites, and much of this can be attributed to the voting rights legislation.

As critics see it, 'the goal of fair representation was grafted onto what was essentially a suffrage law',[8] and despite explicit statements to the contrary by Supreme Court judges, fair representation seems to have been interpreted as proportionate representation. But the arguments used to support this have always been contingent to the history and politics of racism in the USA. No one, to my knowledge, relies on an abstract preference for mirror or descriptive representation; and those most identified with the subsequent evolution of the Voting Rights Act have taken pains to dissociate themselves from any notion that people must be represented by those of their kind. Bernard Grofman puts it thus:

I, like Pitkin, am generally unsympathetic to the mirror view. More specifically, affirmative gerrymandering is, in my view, misconceived if it is seen as a mechanism to guarantee that blacks will be represented by blacks, Hispanics by Hispanics, and whites by whites; rather, the proper use of affirmative gerrymandering is to guarantee that important groups in the population will not be sustantially impaired in their ability to elect representatives *of their choice*.[9]

When the absence of minority politicians is widely perceived as evidence that minorities are *not* electing the representatives of their choice, the distinction might seem disingenuous, but it derives its legitimacy from the stark evidence of racially polarized voting in the USA. The literature on voting rights is full of disturbing evidence of racial bloc voting: that in 1992, for example, there were 24 black representatives in the House of Representatives, but only 3 of these

districts) is less favourable to Latino representation, and that the conditions that most favour the election of Latino politicians are mixed systems which combine some single districts with some at-large voting. See S. Welch, 'The Impact of At-Large Elections on the Representation of Blacks and Hispanics', *Journal of Politics*, 52/4 (1990); also R. de la Garza and L. DeSipio, 'Save the Baby, Change the Bathwater, and Scrub the Tub: Latino Electoral Participation after Seventeen Years of Voting Rights Coverage', *Texas Law Review*, 71/7 (1993).

    [8] T. G. O'Rourke, 'The 1982 Amendment and the Voting Rights Paradox', in Grofman and Davidson, *Controversies in Minority Voting*, 89.

    [9] B. Grofman, 'Should Representatives be Typical of their Constituents?', in B. Grofman, A. Lijphart, R. B. McKay, and H. A. Scarrow (eds.), *Representation and Redistricting Issues* (Lexington, Mass., 1982), 98.

were elected from majority-white congressional districts;[10] that every black politician elected to the state legislatures in Mississippi and Alabama in 1988 was elected from a majority black district[11]; that in all the judicial, legislative, and at-large county office elections in Georgia in 1980–8, 86 per cent of white voters voted for a white candidate and 84 per cent of black voters for a black candidate.[12] When racial bloc voting can be legitimately decribed as 'the single most salient feature of contemporary political life in this country',[13] an exclusive focus on equal rights to register and vote hardly seems a sufficient response.

The increased use of party primaries to identify the candidate for the election has made the polarization particularly apparent, for it is at this stage in the political process that voting preferences are most obviously correlated with race. Once the candidate has been selected, the connection becomes more obscure, for, while white voters are often thought to switch their party allegiances in order to keep out a candidate who is black,[14] black voters tend to support the Democrats regardless. (As former Texas Congressman Mickey Leland reputedly put it, 'Blacks supporting the Republican Party is like a bunch of chickens getting together to support Col. Sanders.'[15]) But the evidence from party primaries, combined with the continued difficulties minority candidates face in getting elected from white-majority constituencies and the very high probability that any black or Latino representative will have been elected by a black or Latino constituency, makes it clear enough that voting in the USA goes by race as well as by party.

But party *is* also relevant, and too much attention to a politics of presence might then seem to threaten the equally pressing politics of ideas. Some critics, for example, have argued that the creation of 'super-majority' black or Latino districts will backfire on minority communities, for, in draining off potential Democratic voters from

[10] Issacharoff, 'Polarized Voting', 1855.

[11] L. McDonald, 'The 1982 Amendments of Section 2 and Minority Representation', in Grofman and Davidson, *Controversies in Minority Voting*, 74.

[12] Ibid. 75. (This covers only cases where there was a serious black candidate, identified as one who got more than half of the black vote.)

[13] Issacharoff, 'Polarized Voting', 1855.

[14] Issacharoff provides a number of examples where the white vote has plummeted on the selection of a black candidate; see ibid. 1854–5.

[15] Cited in ibid. 1878.

surrounding constituencies, they will increase the number of Republican seats. Since the Democrats have been more consistently associated with the pursuit of minority interests, the obsession with minority presence could then come into conflict with the better representation of minority concerns. What is the point of electing more black or Latino Democrats if they are swamped in a sea of Republican opponents?

These arguments are largely empirical, with conflicting evidence marshalled to indicate that redistricting has contributed to an overall increase in the number of Republicans elected,[16] or that the 'gerrymandering skills of Democratic cartographers' have proved sufficient to pre-empt this risk.[17] If the evidence were more definitive, it would have to be taken into account; this is not a debate to be dealt with through unequivocal assertions of what is right or just. We might, with some legitimacy, say that ending a white monopoly over office is an objective that stands on its own, and that even if it carries no additional consequences in increasing the weight attached to minority concerns, it still has an independent symbolic weight. But if the policies pursued by the Democrats were unquestionably more favourable to minority groups than those pursued by the Republicans, and the chances of electing a Democratic majority unquestionably reduced by existing districting arrangements, anyone worried about minority representation would have to regard this as a serious dilemma. (By the same token, if there were only one political party that could be relied on to pursue policies favourable to women, and the adoption of gender quotas made it impossible to get that party elected, any feminist with even one foot on the ground would have to consider short-term compromises of her longer-term aims.) As it happens, the dilemma is not so acute. When one party can be said to take blacks for granted, and the other at best ignore them,[18] the presumed superiority of the Democrats as currently constituted is not so overwhelming. And when the precise effects on

---

[16] A. M. Thernstrom gives a few examples of this in her critical account of the Voting Rights Act, *Whose Votes Count? Affirmative Action and Minority Voting Rights* (Cambridge, Mass., 1987), 234; but her examples are patchy and inconclusive.

[17] B. Grofman and C. Davidson, 'Postcript: What is the Best Route to a Color-Blind Society?' in Grofman and Davidson, *Controversies in Minority Voting*, 314 n.

[18] L. Guinier, 'Keeping the Faith: Black Voters in the Post-Reagan Era', *Harvard Civil Rights—Civil Liberties Law Review*, 24 (1989), 394.

party fortunes are so contested, it is not necessary to dwell long on this point.

I

At its most innocuous, the use of redistricting arrangements to secure more minority representatives has been viewed as a way of representing preferences expressed by groups that are in a permanent minority. In the classic model of European consociational democracy, the minority distinguishes itself from the majority by its persistent preference for a different political party; unless there is some degree of power-sharing between parties, this preference never translates into political influence. In the race-defined politics of the USA, the minority distinguishes itself from the majority by its preference for candidates who come from the minority community; unless there is some modification to the ethnic and racial composition of the legislatures, this preference never achieves any practical result. Put like this, the argument revolves around what is necessary to give all voters a genuinely equal choice. As long as white voters vote for white candidates and black voters for black, it is those who form the racial majority in each district who will get to choose who represents them. The others have little chance of electing the representative 'of their choice'.

Though the case for redistricting is often couched in these judicial terms (many of those who write about minority voting rights have been actively engaged in civil rights' litigation), its critics perceive it as a more tendentious assertion of the politics of presence. Despite repeated disclaimers, there seems to be an underlying presumption that people have to be represented by those of their own kind in order to be well represented; and those most critical of the later developments see the creation of 'safe seats' for minority politicians as a species of legal fixing which undermines the legitimate competition around political ideas. Not that they necessarily defend a white monopoly over legislative assemblies. The most determined critics of voting rights litigation may still acknowledge the desirability of a more racially and ethnically mixed legislature, but any virtue they associate with this is carefully detached from its pretended grounding in political justice or political right.

In her otherwise very critical analysis of voting rights litigation, for example, Abigail Thernstrom recognizes the social and political importance of increasing the proportion of office-holders who are black. But she presents this more as a matter of changing political habits, or providing role models for black Americans. A racially mixed legislature will, she believes, function differently from one that is predominantly white, particularly when the minority representatives are new to the political game, and 'where racially insensitive language and discrimination in the provision of services are long-established political habits'.[19] The election of more black Americans should challenge racial stereotypes, increase the respect for and the self-respect of black voters, and check the more overtly racist practices of white politicians. All this she sees as self-evidently valuable: Thernstrom is not arguing that whites should continue to monopolize political office. But, by narrowing the problem of racism to a matter of bad habits, she seeks to detach it from what she perceives as a misguided rhetoric of minority rights or fair representation. The equal right to vote is simply the equal right to vote, and extending this to include a more spurious 'right to cast an undiluted vote' introduces an illegitimate element of affirmative action into what should be a strictly egalitarian procedure. The evolution of the Voting Rights Act from suffrage law to a way of achieving proportionate representation is then condemned as making some voters count for more than others, for as well as guaranteeing their equal right to register and cast a vote, it secures their additional 'right' to elect representatives of their own kind.

There are two initial points to note against this argument, both of them local instances of arguments developed elsewhere. Most critics of minority rights' litigation insist on a strictly procedural interpretation of political equality, arguing that equality should be tested against input (are all individuals equally enfranchised?) and not against output as well. Political equality is then conceived only as a matter of establishing equality between individuals, and any additional preoccupation with balancing the relative power of different groups is viewed as an illegitimate intrusion on the democratic agenda. But group representation is already built into the political practices of any democracy: as Justice Powell commented in a 1986 voting rights case, '[t]he concept of "representation" necessarily applies to

[19] Thernstrom, *Whose Votes Count?* 239.

groups; groups of voters elect representatives; individuals do not.'[20] Most representation takes place within geographical constituencies, and already presumes some level of shared 'group' interest according to the area where we live. In federal systems which provide formal representation to the constituent states (and equal numbers of representatives to each state, regardless of their population), the practice of group representation has been made even more explicit. Commenting on Canadian political history, Will Kymlicka notes that representation has never been exclusively a matter of the fair representation of individuals, and that there has always been an additional preoccupation with drawing constituency boundaries so as to reflect shared communities of economic, ethnic, religious, environmental, or historical interest.[21] Fair representation is already widely understood as implying more than the equal access of each individual to the vote, and the group interests attached to areas or regions or states already play a significant role.

The second point relates to the ambiguity of equality, and what it means to treat people as equals. Where histories of inequality, deprivation, or exclusion have placed individuals in different relationships to economic resources and political power, we do not treat them equally when we treat them as if they are the same. This is very much what Cass Sunstein has argued in a review of the principle of neutrality in constitutional law. The general ideal of legal neutrality—that the law should not privilege one conception of the good over another, or one group of people over another—has been combined with a far more pernicious doctrine of neutrality in relation to the status quo. 'Decisions that upset existing distributions are treated as "action"; decisions that do not are thought to stay close to nature and thus amount to no action at all.'[22] The result of this, Sunstein argues, is that the law becomes deeply conservative. It tends to regard affirmative action, for example, as illegitimate, because it

[20] Issacharoff, 'Polarized Voting', 1859. See also L. Guinier, 'Groups, Representation, and Race-Conscious Districting: A Case of the Emperor's Clothes', *Texas Law Review*, 71/7 (1993), 1602.

[21] W. Kymlicka, 'Group Representation in Canadian Politics', in F. L. Seidle (ed.), *Equity and Community: The Charter, Interest Advocacy and Representation* (Montreal, 1993); see also W. Kymlicka, *Multicultural Citizenship: A Liberal Theory of Minority Rights* (Oxford, 1995), ch. 7.

[22] C. R. Sunstein, 'Neutrality in Constitutional Law (with Special Reference to Pornography, Abortion and Surrogacy)', *Columbia Law Review*, 92/1 (1992), 2.

treats black people differently from white or women differently from men. In doing this, the law is not just ensuring neutrality; it is making itself neutral between groups that have historically unequal access to resources and power. In the pursuit of equality or neutrality, there are always pertinent questions to be asked about the baseline for assessing equality. Do we take existing, possibly unequal, conditions? Or conditions that might have existed if there had been no such history of inequality? Against a well documented background of racial and ethnic division, we cannot consider political equality as adequately established by the equal right to register for a vote. The underlying presumption of those who want to stand by a more formal equality in voting rights is, in Chandler Davidson's words, 'that minority officeholders answerable to a minority community are dispensable'.[23] This makes it a matter of too little consequence that politicians are overwhelmingly white.

II

The pursuit of minority representation differs from the pursuit of gender parity in a number of significant ways. First, there are the obvious differences in strategy. One operates through pressuring political parties to adopt gender quotas in candidate selection; the other relies on judicial intervention to create more favourable electoral boundaries. To put this in the more hostile language of the critics, one relies on 'safe selecting' and the other on establishing 'safe seats'. This difference is partly pragmatic. Lacking any geographical concentrations of their sex, women cannot resort to a politics of electoral boundaries to secure equality of representation (though they could, in principle, insist on separate electoral registers for women and men). And, faced with the relatively encouraging possibilities that opened up under voting rights legislation, minority groups quite sensibly opted for this rather than the more contested politics of racial quotas. The difference arises as much from these practical considerations of what is possible as from any more theoretically driven contrast between the politics of gender and the politics of race, but it already reveals one potential area of conflict. Women have tended to regard the multi-member constituency as more favourable to gender

---

[23] Davidson, 'The Voting Rights Act', 48.

parity—more easy to shame into action, more amenable to a policy of quotas. Yet most of those pursuing minority representation in the USA have favoured the single-member consitituency over at-large elections. Initial evidence indicates that there is a tension here. Women *do* have better chances of being chosen as candidates in the at-large rather than the single-member system[24]—and if American feminists were ever to adopt gender quotas as their preferred strategy for gender parity, this tension could become more acute.

Beyond this immediate difference of strategy, there are two other major points of comparison with the politics around women's representation. One is that minority voters *are* in a minority. Proportionate presence for women translates into half of the seats, thus potentially half of the power. Proportionate presence for those who are in a numerical minority may end up entirely symbolic; to put this more strongly, it may provide a convenient cover under which the majority continues to deny minority interests and concerns. The strategy of black electoral success could then trade in the goal of protecting minority rights for the more limited achievement of minority presence, and in this trade-off, it could legitimize majority power. As Lani Guinier has noted, the racial polarization in voting is often relocated to a racial polarization in the legislature, with the new black politicians shouldered out of any effective policy role. 'The paradox is that by winning, blacks ultimately lose: as soon as they achieve one electoral success, the focus of the discrimination shifts to the legislative arena.'[25] Where this happens, the policy outcomes may be entirely unaffected by the changing composition of the legislature. Mere presence may be detached from many of the reasons why it was thought to matter.

The second point of comparison is that the political claims of black (and, somewhat less so, Latino) Americans are more consistently grounded in perceptions of a distinct group identity and interest, and as such are conceived as more threatening to social cohesion. The historical experience of slavery; the continuing and grotesque disparities between black and white Americans in levels of poverty,

---

[24] S. Welch and D. T. Studlar, 'Multi-Member Districts and the Representation of Women: Evidence from Britain and the United States', *Journal of Politics*, 52/2 (1990), 394.
[25] L. Guinier, 'No Two Seats: The Elusive Quest for Political Equality', *Virginia Law Review*, 77/8 (1991), 1447.

unemployment, educational qualifications, housing conditions, drug abuse, prison sentences, and infant mortality; the often stark geographic separation between black and white communities—all these combine to create a very different context from the power struggles between women and men. The latter look comparatively benign, not only because women tend to live with 'the enemy', but because it has been so hard to conceive of women as forming a single cohesive bloc. Despite occasional intimations of a gender gap on questions of welfare and warfare, women are not easily defined by a consistently 'female' perspective—and, as Hege Skjeie has shown us, this is equally true even in cultures that exhibit a strong sense of women's difference from men.[26] In contrast to this, the representation of minority Americans derives much of its legitimacy from the perception of clearly defined group interests that have been historically denied.

Black Americans have been considerably more forthcoming than women in defining themselves as members of a distinct group,[27] and when this is combined with a voting rights strategy that works through the geographical separation between majority and minority commmunities, it raises a spectre that rarely hovers over debates on more women in politics. In a society that is already divided, the creation of black-majority districts may be said to make the boundaries between majority and minority communities even more impermeable. The fear of balkanization then looms large, and the tension between race-neutral or race-conscious strategies becomes more acute than the comparable tension between sex-neutral and sex-conscious approaches. In the debate over gender quotas, critics have typically concentrated on the way these undermine the status of women politicians, and have argued that the women who achieve their position via quotas will have less credibility than those who fight their way up through a 'sex-neutral' game. Though similar arguments frequently surface in debates about racial quotas or minority representation in the USA, these have combined with a more troubled sense of the risks to political cohesion when divided communities are made still more distinct.

[26] H. Skjeie, 'The Rhetoric of Difference: On Women's Inclusion into Political Elites', *Politics and Society*', 19/2 (1991).

[27] One of the main findings of Katherine Tate's *From Protest to Politics* is that this group identification by black Americans remains extremely high.

Recent court rulings have brought this very explicitly to the fore, and have set significant limits to what can be done through future redistricting arrangements. In a particularly important judgment in the 1993 Shaw *v.* Reno case, the Supreme Court objected to a 'bizarrely' shaped congressional district in North Carolina, which wound along 160 miles of an interstate highway to take in the urban centres where black voters were most likely to live. There was no suggestion that the redistricting plan unfairly privileged black voters over white: its relatively modest aim was to ensure that two of North Carolina's twelve members of Congress would be black, in a state in which the black population is 22 per cent. But the boundaries had no obvious justification other than to generate a black majority district, and it was this that became the crux of the argument. Amid accusations of 'political apartheid'—that voters were being separated simply on the basis of their race—the proposed redistricting was struck down.

The judgment goes against a long history of previous judgments which had regarded a disproportionality between the number of black voters and the number of black representatives as relevant to the case; as Lani Guinier puts it, it seems to shift the debate almost to the terrain of aesthetics, and to whether the shape of the district looks right.[28] A certain amount of tinkering with boundaries may, by implication, still be acceptable. No district is simply shaped by nature, and in the margins between one shape and another courts might legitimately consider their racial effect. But anything that diverges too markedly from what is deemed geographically 'natural' now lays itself open to charges of racial gerrymandering. This leaves the strategy of voting rights litigation in rather a quandary. Nearly all majority-black districts currently elect black representatives, but the proportion still hovers around 2 per cent of total elected offices. There is limited scope for further extension if all districts have to 'look right', for while the geographical concentration of minority voters has produced many 'natural' constituencies, there is no hope of approximating proportionate representation through redistricting strategies alone. As Katherine Tate notes, 'most expect future Black politicians to emerge from districts where Blacks are only a minority of the voters':[29] not that people are greatly optimistic

---

[28] Guinier, 'Groups, Representation and Race-Conscious Districting', 1593 n.
[29] Tate, *From Protest to Politics*, 178.

about the prospects for this, but that no other route is available, given the way populations are dispersed. The use of redistricting arrangements to raise the number of minority representatives may now have reached its historical limit.

Against this background, it is tempting to argue that the strategy of voting rights litigation has proved itself misguided. With hindsight, one might say that the pursuit of minority representation has relied *implicitly* on a notion of quotas (the presumption that minority Americans are ill represented as long as their numbers in legislative assemblies are disproportionate to their numbers in the population as a whole), but has failed to justify itself on this basis. Previous successes were arguably based on a fudge, with districts that were undoubtedly designed with some quota in mind, but not explicitly defended in such terms. Any redistricting proposal that can be shown to be motivated *only* by quota concerns is then inherently vulnerable: it will be dismissed as 'bizarre', 'unnatural', unaesthetic. If the underlying objective is to achieve a more proportionate quota of minority communities, it might have been better to develop rigorous arguments in favour of this.

This conclusion has considerable logical attraction, but does not really engage with the realities of American politics, or the differences between gender and race. I have already indicated one of these differences, which relates to the degree of separation between different groups. However acute the conflicts between women and men, these can never lend themselves to any serious scenario of separation or secession—if for no other reason than that women have fathers and sons, and men have mothers and daughters. The history of racism, by contrast, can and does lend itself to stark separations between different communities; and the history of apartheid, in particular, has made the use of racial quotas in politics far more controversial than the use of quotas for women and men. Not that this is definitive: pragmatic assessments about what is politically acceptable often favour the less radical option, even when alternatives could be usefully pursued. But racial quotas carry with them very different historical associations from gender quotas, and we cannot just set aside historical meanings in the name of abstract logic.

Gender is also a much simpler category, building on immediately visible differences between women and men. Race and ethnicity are far more contested, and while it is relatively easy to draw a distinction between majority and minority communities, the latter always subdivides into a number of minorities which may not regard themselves as well represented by members of another minority group. The category of non-white Americans spans African Americans, Asian Americans, Latino Americans (the last breaking down into further distinctions according to country of origin), as well as a wide variety of smaller ethnic groups. The category of non-white Britons covers the major distinction between Afro-Caribbeans and Asians (the latter subdividing into those of Indian, Pakistani, Bangladeshi, or East African origin), as well as a further multiplicity of other ethnic groups. This complex formation is less obviously amenable to a politics of quotas than the distinction between women and men. Distinguishing only between whites and the rest produces a crude and misleading distinction, and it is hard to find the appropriate balance between this simplistic racial dualism and a more sophisticated—but potentially unworkable—*series* of quotas which captures the multiplicity of ethnic groups. Again, this does not mean that ethnic quotas are always and everywhere impossible, but it goes some way towards explaining the greater acceptability of quotas by gender.

III

In considering the arguments over minority representation in the USA, the crucial starting point is that this is not a debate that divides into simple either/or camps. As Chandler Davidson has noted, there are at least three major strands in play. These include what he calls the 'narrow constructionists', who value the Voting Rights Act only in so far as it dealt with inequities in the right to vote, but reject the later emphasis on achieving racial proportionality in elected assemblies; the 'standpatters', who support the subsequent interpretations and want to continue the good work along these lines; and the 'expansive constructionists', who share with the standpatters their commitment to a politics of presence, but want to develop this in ways that will enhance the conditions for multi-racial coalition, and tackle many serious misgivings over a politics of 'authentic' representation.[30]

---

[30] Davidson, 'The Voting Rights Act'.

Within this more complex division of the field, there is virtually no problem raised by the first group that has not been addressed in some way by the third. Supporters of voting rights legislation have not been backward in voicing their criticisms of the politics of presence, and some of the most acute judgments on its limits and dangers come from those who regard political presence as a necessary but insufficient condition. The arguments may have been more convoluted than those that underpin the case for gender quotas, but in the process they have engaged very directly with the relationship between presence and ideas. In particular, they have dwelt extensively on that familiar tension between who and what is to be represented.

The emphasis on 'who' tends towards essentialized definitions of each group, which are then presumed to have a fixed and unified group interest. This does little justice to their own internal differentiation, or to the historically changing character of each social group. Race or ethnicity can then become a symbolic shorthand which obscures other areas of difference and erases other aspects of political choice. In the absence of a clearly defined and shared group interest which any member would automatically promote, changing the character of the representatives may then change nothing else. If the commitment to raising the proportion of minority representatives went no further than a notion of equal opportunities at a political career, this problem would be less pressing. But those pursuing the goal of minority political presence have always perceived it in relation to the policy changes that will follow from this. This is not a tension they are inclined to ignore.

The presumption of unity will look more or less plausible depending on the group in question. It carries greater conviction as applied to black Americans, for example, than to the more diverse grouping of Latino Americans, for the latter come from different countries of origin and very different experiences of migration. In the absence of a self-perceived common political agenda among Latinos, the creation of Latino majority districts may be particularly misguided, and some have argued that the more appropriate enabling device is simply the provision of bilingual electoral information to raise overall political participation.[31] But even where there is a stronger history of

---

[31] This is argued, for example, in de la Garza and DeSipio, 'Save the Baby'.

group identification, it is hardly legitimate to see this as overriding everything else. The very great income divide in the USA between black professionals and what William J. Wilson has called the 'truly disadvantaged'[32] makes this particularly risky, for any exclusive emphasis on changing the racial and ethnic composition of political élites can cover up significant differences within what is not really a black 'community'. In his analysis of black urban regimes, Adolf Reed argues that the only initiatives that have benefited the entire black community are those that have reduced the incidence of police brutality; apart from this, the attachment to progrowth or employment policies has had very differential class impact on the black interests they supposedly promote. But through 'the legerdemain of symbolic racial collectivism',[33] this differential impact has been disguised or defused: benefits that accrue to any member of the group are presented as if they were benefits to all. The easy equation of more minority representatives with better representation of minority interests only makes sense against a homogeneous community of interests, and neither Latino nor black Americans really fit this picture.

Part of what is at issue here is the asymmetry already noted in the general arguments about political presence. The absence of certain categories of people—whether these be women or Latinos or blacks—testifies to a significant difference in interests, for it is hard to explain such patterns of exclusion without recourse to either intentional or structural discrimination. But, failing an essentialist definition of unified group identities and interests, there is no guarantee that changing the composition of political élites will change the substance of representation. The legitimate concern over minority under-representation can then become a more limited vehicle for promoting the career interests of minority politicians. This can be additionally defended for its symbolic or social effects—I would agree with Guinier, for example, that '[b]lacks cannot enjoy equal dignity and political status until black representatives join the

[32] W. J. Wilson, *The Truly Disadvantaged: The Inner City, the Underclass, and Public Policy* (Chicago, 1987). Income inequality is greater among black households than among white, and has increased at a faster rate between 1966 and 1981.

[33] A. Reed, 'The Black Urban Regime: Structural Origins and Consequences', *Comparative Urban and Community Research*, 1 (1988), 167.

council of government'[34]—but even in combination with this, it falls far short of the original intent.

Much of the subsequent discussion has rightly focused around the problem of political accountability—and implicitly, at least, the gap that can open up between a politics of presence and a politics of ideas. In the idealized conventions of the politics of ideas, candidates will present themselves to an electorate on the basis of their policies and programmes. They will have to defend these in the course of their campaign, and make visible efforts to implement them after their successful election. One of the worries about the strategy of 'safe seats' for minority representatives is that the politicians may not even bother to cloak themselves in any garb of political ideas. The presumption of authentic, or what Adolf Reed calls 'organic', representation[35] can then reduce the vitality of political debate. When the policies most appropriate to equalizing majority and minority communities are so contested—and so very far from obvious—this is not a desirable result.

As Lani Guinier has argued in her extensive critique of 'the theory of black electoral success',[36] the exclusive focus on securing more black representatives encourages the belief that black politicians *are* representative merely by virtue of being black. Issues of accountability drop out of the picture, and this is partly because of 'the message already conveyed to black elected officials by the authenticity assumption', which seems to relieve them of the burden of 'developing appropriate agendas or articulating community demands'.[37] In the more ambitious visions of the 1950s and 1960s, civil rights activists thought that increasing black political participation would be a way of transforming American politics and setting out a new social justice agenda. They also believed it would cut through the

[34] Guinier, 'Keeping the Faith', 421.

[35] Reed introduces this concept in his discussion of *The Jesse Jackson Phenomenon* (New Haven, 1986), where he argues that Jackson contested the 1984 presidential nomination on 'a premise of unmediated representation of a uniform racial totality', (p. 35). Basing his claims on the grounds of an organic relationship and supposed popular acclamation that was never put to any test, Jackson barely bothered even to set out a programme.

[36] See the essays collected in L. Guinier, *The Tyranny of the Majority* (New York, 1994); see also L. Guinier, 'Voting Rights and Democratic Theory: Where Do We Go from Here?' in Grofman and Davidson, *Controversies in Minority Voting*.

[37] L. Guinier 'The Triumph of Tokenism: The Voting Rights Act and the Theory of Black Success', *Michigan Law Review*, 89/5 (1991).

older patronage system, in which white politicians could pick and choose those they considered 'leaders' of the black community, forcing them to deal instead with representatives chosen by the people. Though Guinier is very much committed to the goal of black political presence, she argues that the exclusive emphasis on numbers generates a non-democratic notion of racial authenticity, and that this makes it far more difficult for the voters to get their desired policies in place.

The strategy of 'safe seats' for black or Latino representatives also threatens to diminish political participation and political involvement: this is a point repeatedly made by critics and supporters alike. Timothy O'Rourke sees the development of the Voting Rights Act into a strategy for raising the number of minority representatives as a misguided application of the 'Guardian Ethic', where people have become 'more concerned with fixing the results than with improving the politics that gives rise to the results', and have focused all their attention on legal rather than political action.[38] In a more sympathetic review of the effects of voting rights legislation on the political participation of Latino Americans, Rodolfo de la Garza and Louis DeSipio also stress that politics can fall out of the picture.[39] The creation of majority–minority districts usually has a 'dampening effect on electoral participation',[40] for, after that first moment of intense competition when the districts are initially established, they become safe seats for the existing incumbents, who no longer need to mobilize their local support. This has particularly disturbing consequences for Latino Americans, whose participation remains at substantially lower levels than the white electorate. It also, more generally, threatens to relieve elected politicians from any continued responsibility for developing and defending their programmes. If the communities being represented did indeed share a homogeneous group identity, this might not so much matter (or might matter only to those who independently value political involvement). But when the communities are self-evidently diverse in their interests and goals, any decline in citizen participation reduces the means of keeping politicians to account.

---

[38] O'Rourke, 'The 1982 Amendment and the Voting Rights Paradox', 112.
[39] de la Garza and DeSipio, 'Save the Baby'.   [40] Ibid. 1514.

IV

The dangers in presuming a unified group interest or identity are widely discussed in the literature, and a number of recent contributions tread a difficult course between stressing group difference and resisting the implication of group identity. Kathryn Abrams, for example, uses the extensive evidence of racially polarized voting to insist that majority and minority racial groups not only vote for different candidates, but also differ in their substantive preferences and goals.[41] But this is not, she stresses, 'to suggest that all members of particular racial minority groups have similar perspectives on questions of political importance, or that a legacy of discrimination—according to race, gender, or any other immutable characteristic—shapes the consciousness or political perspectives of all group members in the same way'.[42] Lani Guinier makes a similar distinction, for while she sees racial group representation as required by the deep racial cleavages in American society, and regards black voters as a discrete social category with their own distinctive and disadvantaged perspective,[43] she seeks to detach this from any presumption of a unified group identity. '[R]acial groups are not monolithic, nor are they necessarily cohesive';[44] their racial self-identity is cut across by divisions of gender or age or class; they may agree on civil rights issues, but disagree sharply on other concerns. Racial groups still need representation, but this is best achieved, Guinier argues, in ways 'that permit automatic, self-defined apportionment based on shifting political or cultural affiliation and interests'.[45] This is why she argues for electoral systems based on proportional representation.

The distinction between group difference and group identity will be far more palatable to those who wish to steer clear of essential or unified identity, but it also threatens to undermine the simplicity of the original case. Once the case for minority group representation is detached from the stronger version of minority group interest— which it surely has to be, for empirical and analytic reasons alike—it

---

[41] K. Abrams, 'Relationships of Representation in Voting Rights Act Jurisprudence', *Texas Law Review*, 71/7 (1993).
[42] Ibid. 1433 n.   [43] Guinier, 'Triumph of Tokenism', 1105–8.
[44] Guinier, 'Groups, Representation and Race-Conscious Districting', 1622.
[45] Ibid.

loses some of its initial force. In the parallel case of gender parity, the instability of 'women's interests' shifted the argument away from a strictly instrumental pursuit of agreed and pre-determined interest and towards a more open-ended project of articulating silenced perspectives and changing political agendas. This hardly seems sufficiently hard-hitting as applied to black or Latino Americans, where the representation of distinct and denied interest still registers as the major concern. Many of those pursuing the goal of minority representation now combine a strong sense of group interests with an equally strong sense of the groups as composing themselves around shifting and divided concerns. On the face of it, this looks rather incoherent.

The only way out of this impasse is to seek out a different balance between presence and ideas. A greater element of policy-related competition has to be introduced into what are otherwise uncontested safe seats, for, unless there is more explicit political debate and choice, the representatives will be 'representative' only in a mirror or descriptive sense. This argument applies, *a fortiori*, to the growing trend towards 'super-majority' districts, where minority voters make up more than 60 per cent of the voting population. One recently developed alternative is what has come to be known as 'modified at-large election': to return to multi-member districts with at-large election, but simultaneously to reduce the electoral threshold so that any candidate can be elected on an appropriate proportion of the total votes. In this system, voters would have as many votes as there are seats, and under conditions of cumulative voting they could choose to cast all these for a single candidate. The minimalist strategy would be to sacrifice influence over most of the seats and concentrate on getting at least one minority representative elected. This would hardly differ in its effects from current districting arrangements; nor would it significantly modify the tendency towards 'authentic' representation. But the proposed alternative would also open up space for a different kind of electoral strategy. There would be an increased incentive for all candidates (whatever their political or racial identification) to seek support from more than one community, and this would encourage them to set out platforms that address minority as well as majority concerns. One very considerable benefit would be increased political involvement, and more sustained debate between a range of priorities and concerns.

This proposal might also, as Lani Guinier suggests, reduce potential conflicts between the representation of race and the representation of gender.'[L]owering the threshold of exclusion potentially empowers all numerically significant groups, including minority political parties, organized groups of women, the elderly, as well as any group of working class or poor people presently politically disadvantaged under a majoritarian model.'[46]

In subsequent developments of this argument, Guinier has moved even more decisively on to the terrain of proportional representation. Any form of winner-takes-all districting 'aggregates people by virtue of assumptions about their group characteristics and then inflates the winning group's power by allowing it to represent all voters in a regional unit'.[47] Those who recoil in horror from race-conscious districting are being distinctly disingenuous about the gerrymandering that goes into any kind of districting; and those who query the claim of black representatives to represent all 'their' black constituents are overlooking the equally suspect presupposition that any candidate who wins represents all those who voted for another. The answer, she argues, lies in a system of proportional representation in which everybody's vote counts for somebody's election. As far as racial group representation is concerned, this has the great advantage of recognising self-defined rather than essentialized groups. Race-conscious districting 'may be rigidly essentialist, presumptuously isolating, or politically divisive'.[48] In contrast to this, modified at-large elections would enable racial groups to define themselves around what are shifting communities of interest. Difference need no longer be enshrined in the fixing of electoral boundaries. 'Modified at-large election systems encourage continuous redistricting by the voters themselves based on the way they cast their votes in each election.'[49]

The theoretical basis on which Guinier grounds this is not entirely secure: it claims that '[o]ne-vote, one-value is realized when everyone's vote counts for someone's election';[50] and it then lays itself perilously open to Brian Barry's comments on the 'palpably fallacious reasoning' behind a discourse of 'wasted votes'. In recent years, Barry notes,

[46] Guinier, 'The Triumph of Tokenism', 1151.
[47] Guinier, 'Groups, Representation, and Race-Conscious Districting',1593.
[48] Ibid. 1624.   [49] Ibid. 1638.   [50] Ibid. 1594.

supporters of systems of proportional representation in Britain have succeeded in scoring something of a propaganda victory by pressing the idea that the vote for a candidate who comes third (or lower) in a plurality system is 'wasted' and the people who vote for the candidate are 'effectively disenfranchised'. But then why stop there? The only way of making sense of this argument is by postulating that anyone who voted for a candidate other than the actual winner—even the runner-up—was 'effectively disenfranchised' . . . I do not think that anyone of ordinary intelligence would be found saying of an election for, say, the post of president of a club: "I didn't vote for the winning candidate. In other words my vote didn't help elect anybody. And that means I was effectively disenfranchised.'[51]

Clearly, there *is* a problem with defining political equality in terms of an equal chance of voting for the winning candidate. There might be all kinds of reasons (including the craziness of the candidate's politics) why the person I vote for has no hope of being elected, and I can hardly complain that this outcome is a blot on political equality. But the argument for proportional representation does not normally rest on a principle of individual equality that gives all citizens the same 'right' to get their candidates elected. It is more commonly defended as a way of making the representative body more 'representative' of citizen opinion. It considers political equality in terms of some roughly proportionate representation of political preference and opinion, which is hardly the same as saying that all preferences should have an equal chance of being adopted. Minority preferences should get minority representation; majority preferences should get majority representation. It is rather an odd stretching of this notion to interpret it as saying that there should be no difference in the way minorities and majorities are treated.

I see no problem in detaching Guinier's strong arguments against winner-takes-all representation from their more doubtful underpinning in every individual's right to elect someone of his/her choice. Her great strength, in this context, is the way she negotiates the terrain between recognizing that there *are* distinct group interests, but that these are neither fixed nor guaranteed by essential identities, and the way she then detaches the claim to racial group representation from its dangerous grounding in racial authenticity. The emphasis throughout is on maintaining the importance of racially mixed

---

[51] B. Barry, 'Is Democracy Special?' in P. Laslett and J. Fishkin (eds.), *Philosophy, Politics and Society*, (Oxford, 1979), 158.

legislatures, while strengthening the accountability of representatives via their programmes and policies and ideas. Presence is not privileged over ideas; ideas are not privileged over presence. In the racially polarized politics of the USA, the priority is to combine these two.

V

The less ambitious alternative has been to press for a combination of 'safe seats' to sustain the number of minority representatives, plus a larger number of more mixed constituencies that will promote more active political debate. This is part of what de la Garza and DeSipio argue in their assessment of Latino electoral participation;[52] it is also what Kathryn Abrams argues in her rather grand attempt to marry ideals of republican citizenship with the tricky details of electoral reform.[53] For de la Garza and DeSipio, the priority is to raise levels of political participation and involvement by making the politics more contested, and they argue for more 'Latino-influence' districts as a way of achieving this effect. For Abrams, the priority is to develop a more 'interactive participation' in which people come to appreciate common interests and concerns.

In both instances, there is a clear determination not to propose anything that might reduce the existing number of black or Latino representatives. Thus, Abrams argues that democracy should not be viewed just as the aggregation of preferences expressed through the ballot box, but as something that actively promotes co-operation and mutual understanding. As applied to minority representation, this suggests that the best measures are those that enhance co-operation across difference, and Abrams sees the logic of her position as implying a maximum number of districts where majority and minority voters are evenly balanced. This might, however, reverse past gains in minority representation, and what she proposes instead is a pluralist approach to boundary decisions. Some districts should be drawn so as to secure safe seats around concentrations of minority voters; others should be created where minority voters make up 40 per cent of the electorate. In these latter, there would be an incentive to political co-operation between majority and minority com-

---

[52]   de la Garza and DeSipio, 'Save the Baby'.
[53]   Abrams, ' "Raising Politics Up" ', 477.

munities, which might actually increase the number of blacks or Latinos elected. But even if it had no such effect, the creation of more mixed constituencies could promote democratic dialogue and help voters identify areas of common concern. Continuing gains in political presence would then be combined with a transformative politics that encourages interconnection: a fuller and fairer democracy brought about by different districting arrangements.

This is 'political fixing' with a vengeance, and most European observers will probably regard it as a distinctly odd translation of high theories of civic republicanism into detailed recommendations to boundary commissions. The more important point, however, is that the argument backs away from what might seem its logical conclusions. The strategy of safe seats is found distinctly wanting, but, failing any alternative guarantee of racially mixed government, it has been hard to drop it entirely. The history of racial exclusions, combined with the disturbing evidence of racially polarized voting, continue to put a premium on measures that will increase the number of representatives elected from and by minority communities. So far it is the strategy of majority–minority districting that has done most to achieve this end. There is considerable—and very legitimate—reluctance to give up on what Samuel Issacharoff describes as 'a limited but real step forward'.[54] The limits are widely acknowledged, but, in the absence of a convincing alternative that successfully integrates ideas with presence, many feel obliged to fudge the full implications of their critique. Attention then turns to ways of combining the existing safe seats with additional districts in which minorities can exert an 'influence', or where majorities and minorities will be more evenly balanced.

In comparison with this, Lani Guinier's proposals are more obviously consistent, for she just drops black majority districts altogether. But her preferred option may not be available in contemporary America, where proportional representation is regarded with deep suspicion, and where the real choice may remain between race-conscious and race-neutral districting.[55] Where this is

---

[54] Issacharoff, 'Polarized Voting', 1891.

[55] Guinier notes one example where an at-large system and semi-proportional voting was adopted—and actually increased the number of black representatives elected—but was later overturned by the circuit judges, who reimposed single-district arrangements: 'Groups, Representation and Race-Conscious Districting', 1636.

so, it becomes necessary to weave a more compromised course between the conflicting demands of ideas and presence. Assessments of voting rights litigation always involve consequentialist judgments on likely possibilities and outcomes: this can never be just a matter of high principle, but also of anticipated effects. Pragmatic judgments are, in that sense, inevitable, for there may be no currently viable option that can combine all legitimate concerns. To return to an earlier point, it might be argued that the case for minority representation would move on to surer ground if it adopted an explicit policy of quotas. But when racial quotas in politics are so intrinsically fraught, such a development might reverse the existing gains. When political theory meets up with practical policy, there has to be some attention to what is possible or likely.

VI

The remaining problem revolves around the fact that minorities *are* in a minority. If minority representation is ultimately grounded in the need for better representation of minority group interest(s), then the solution hardly matches up to the problem, for it is entirely possible to have a 'descriptively' correct legislature in which white majorities continue to rule. This possibility is a long way off, for proportionality is nowhere near being achieved; but even if it became reality it would not guarantee policy change. Minorities would have more of a platform from which to press their case, and if they worked in multi-racial coalition they could expect at least some minor concessions. But the power attached to their presence depends ultimately on moral force: that being there somehow 'shames' others into recognizing they have a case.

David Estlund has argued that 'the goal of greater minority representation at the legislative and policy levels can be endorsed from either a deliberative or strategic point of view'.[56] The strategic point of view treats politics primarily as a matter of economic rationality, and sees increasing the number of minority representatives as necessary to the pursuit of minority interest. Despite considerable qualms about what gets smuggled into 'minority group interest', this

[56] D. M. Estlund, 'Who's Afraid of Deliberative Democracy? On the Strategic/Deliberative Dichotomy in Recent Constitutional Jurisprudence', *Texas Law Review*, 71/7 (1993), 1473.

remains the dominant approach in voting rights literature. Connections have, however, been forged with theories of deliberative democracy (Kathryn Abrams's work is one obvious example of this), and Estlund sees this as by far the more promising route.

The central premiss of deliberative democracy is that there is more to politics than the aggregation of individual or group interest, and that the extra in question has a clear normative edge. Theorists of deliberative democracy refuse to restrict themselves to a vision of politics as the expression of existing preference or interest: partly, as the work of Cass Sunstein indicates, because limiting the choice to currently expressed preference cuts out what people might have wanted if they had been able to perceive the wider range of possible options;[57] but also, as Estlund emphasizes, because theorists of deliberative democracy seek out independent ethical standards for evaluating political practice. Hence the strange tendency he observes among deliberative democrats to identify themselves with the work of John Rawls—despite the marked absence of any kind of deliberation from Rawls's account of political justice. The answer to this conundrum, Estlund suggests, lies precisely in Rawls's indifference to the messy realities of politics. Because Rawls's theory of justice 'supplies a standard for the evaluation of political practice that is independent of actual political choice procedures',[58] his work has won many admirers among those who query existing patterns of political choice. Estlund goes on to argue that the case for minority representation is more securely based in a deliberative than a strategic perspective. Because minorities *are* in a minority, they need something other than evidence of racial exclusion to challenge white majority rule. Unless they additionally challenge the very legitimacy of majority rule in majority interest, they will be left with little more than a few seats in the governing assembly.

The implication of this argument is that equal or proportionate presence has to be seen as an enabling condition for something other than the representation of interest. The point is not just that certain interests have been left out, and now need to be added to the picture: if that were the only thing at issue, the change could prove merely cosmetic. The point, rather, is that the exclusion of certain interests

---

[57] C. R. Sunstein, 'Preferences and Politics', *Philosophy and Public Affairs*, 20/1 (1991).
[58] Estlund, 'Who's Afraid of Deliberative Democracy?', 1463.

and perspectives and concerns has legitimized illegitimate practices, and that their subsequent inclusion is a necessary condition for getting others to re-evaluate their previous bias. But bias can only be acknowledged as a problem from a perspective other than representing interest. As long as politics is perceived as the rational pursuit of individual or group interest, no one group is in a much of position to complain of another group's bias: bias is simply the name of the game—we all go for what is in our best interests. The interest-driven model allows no space for normative judgments on racist bigotry or bias. What are the minorities to say when they are consistently—but democratically—outvoted? Too easy an endorsement of politics as the pursuit of individual or group-based interest could leave previously excluded minorities stranded in their subsequent inclusion, for it provides no outlet if the majorities continue to rule in their own interest.

In a relatively confident reading of urban politics in America, Browning, Marshall, and Tabb argue that the most promising developments in minority representation have occurred where minorities have been able to rely on white liberal support, and that it is the politics of bi-racial coalition, rather than separatism, that has most empowered minority communities.[59] In a later study, they put the point more strongly. It is not just that minorities *are* minorities, and cannot then translate their proportionate presence in assemblies into significant policy influence; they may not even begin to approximate this proportionality where there is no evidence of white liberal support.[60] Minority voters are most likely to turn out and vote when they can see some chance of their representatives participating in governing groups. Where getting more black or Latino politicians elected is going to be largely symbolic, levels of mobilization tend to drop. People vote when they think it will matter—and it matters most where there is some chance of white liberal support.

This offers a relatively optimistic scenario—for these governing coalitions of majorities and minorities have indeed emerged. The more discouraging edge is that, even when minority politicians come to form part of a governing coalition, this often coincides with a

[59] R. P. Browning, D. R. Marshall and D. H. Tabb, *Protest Is Not Enough: The Struggle of Blacks and Hispanics for Equality in Urban Politics* (Berkeley, 1984).

[60] R. P. Browning, D. R. Marshall and D. H. Tabb, (eds.), *Racial Politics in American Cities* (New York, 1990).

paralysis in policy. One of the more striking developments of the last two decades has been the emergence of the black urban regimes, where black politicians—sometimes as a straightforward majority, but more often in coalition with white or Latino Democrats—have captured control of some of America's largest cities. This development owes as much to demographic and structural changes as to the operation of the Voting Rights Act, and these structural changes have then tied the hands of the new city governments.[61] The black population of the cities has increased, while the white population has declined. (This partly reflects the relocation of manufacturing outside the cities, but also the depressing dynamic between black migration to the cities and white migration to the suburbs.) Black administrations have then been elected to power just at that moment when welfare pressures go up and tax receipts go down. As Adolf Reed puts it, 'the dynamics that make possible the empowerment of black regimes are the same as those that produce the deepening marginalization and dispossession of a substantial segment of the urban black population'.[62]

Annexation of the suburbs offers one way out of this impasse—and would in many ways be fairer, given that suburban dwellers make use of the city, but contribute little to the city's costs. But this would not only be vigorously contested by white residents in the suburbs; it would also conflict with the goals of black representation. '[G]iven patterns of racial voting, elected officials and aspirants to officialdom in black majority or near-majority cities are understandably loath to annex pockets of potentially antagonistic white voters.'[63] Achieving a more equitable distribution of the costs of running a city comes up against the equally pressing concern with a more equitable distribution of representative office; as is repeatedly noted in the literature, gains in political presence can coincide with an inability to do anything with the power.

I shall return to the relationship between group representation and deliberative democracy in Chapter 6, where I argue a strong compatibility between these potentially divergent approaches, but take issue with suggestions that interest could drop out of the picture. The point to stress from this chapter is that the meaning of group identity and interest has been exhaustively addressed in the

---

[61] Reed, 'The Black Urban Regime'.   [62] Ibid. 148.   [63] Ibid. 141.

literature on minority voting rights. Opponents of race-conscious districting often focus on the way it threatens to subdivide what is already a pretty divided society, and they have evoked the fears of separatism or balkanization which so often surround the development of a politics of presence. Though these fears are not entirely unwarranted, the preoccupation with 'political apartheid' seriously underestimates the desire for political *inclusion* that is the real impetus to any politics of presence. The preoccupation also elevates considerations of political stability above what counts as fair representation, and employs the first to disparage moves towards the second. In contrast to this rather all-or-nothing approach, those promoting measures to raise the number of minority representatives have occupied a more complex and nuanced terrain. As this chapter has already established, they have been more than willing to acknowledge unintended consequences of past developments—the fall-off in political participation, the attenuated accountability of minority politicians—and they have been very concerned to dislodge essentialist presumptions about what characterizes the excluded groups. In the process, they have explored a variety of further modifications that could promote more active policy debate. What most characterizes these explorations is their complex interweaving of the politics of ideas with the politics of presence.

The case for minority representation in the USA derives its most immediate power from the perception of distinct and different group interests that have been historically denied. But too simplistic a notion of what constitutes a group hardly fits the more complex reality; it also lends itself too readily to ideas of authentic or organic representation, which can discourage developments around policy and ideas. If achieving a more proportionate representation of minority politicians were of merely symbolic significance, this might not so much matter. But when it is allied with expectations of new policy directions, these constraints become more pressing. The American example thus confirms the dangers of setting up an either/or choice between ideas and presence, and the importance of maintaining the relationship between these two.

CHAPTER 5

————

Canada and the challenge
of inclusion

In the examples so far considered, the problem of political exclusion has generated a solution through political presence, and the main areas of contention have revolved around the status of the proposed representatives, and the sense in which they can claim to be representatives of 'their' group. There is always the additional anxiety, hovering uneasily in the background, over who qualifies as an excluded group, and always some version of that 'slippery slope' conundrum which asks, if gender, why not ethnicity? if race, why not language? if any of these, why not class? Supporters of gender parity have had a relatively easy ride with this, for when women make up half the population, and are additionally dispersed across all the relevant distinctions of class or ethnicity or language, achieving parity for women hardly forecloses the representation of other aspects of political identity. Supporters of minority representation in the USA have had to acknowledge at least one legitimate parallel, as in the 1975 amendment to the Voting Rights Act which extended it to cover the under-representation of Latino as well as black Americans. But in both instances there seemed good enough grounds for highlighting just one or two aspects of political exclusion. The Nordic countries, which took the lead in introducing gender quotas, are widely known for their ethnic (if not linguistic) homogeneity, and this helped expose the gender imbalance in elected assemblies as the outstanding problem of democratic equality. In the far more heterogeneous society of the USA, the widely shared perception of race as *the* major social divide helped support a politics which viewed this as the dominant political exclusion; despite the later extension to deal with the historically disadvantaged Latino population, the main emphasis is still on a black–white racial divide. In both these contexts, it was possible to abstract one (or two) out of many available axes of political exclusion, and this simplification of the field is part of what has sustained a politics of presence.

Canadian politics has proved itself less amenable to any such strategy of abstraction, for, while the challenge of political inclusion is both acute and extensively debated, the very diversity of the significant 'differences' has militated against any exclusive emphasis on political presence. Relatively open immigration policies have created a multi-ethnic and multicultural country, and Canada now contains an active politics around multiculturalism, as well as strong feminist initiatives to raise the status of women in politics. This is superimposed, however, on the as yet unresolved relationship between the 'three founding peoples': the Aboriginal peoples, who were overrun and displaced by initially French and later British settlement; the minority French-speaking settlers, who were incorporated (by conquest) into a British colony; and the dominant English-speaking majority. The 1867 British North American Act established a federal system of government with some degree of autonomy for the French-Canadian province of Quebec, while the 1876 Indian Act established a quasi-colonial system of land reserves for status Indians and their descendants, all of them situated well away from the towns. Some of the most pressing divisions within Canadian society then coincide with broadly territorial units, and this lends itself more readily to demands for self-government, special status, or secession.

Not that demands for equal or proportionate presence have been lacking. In the debates concerning the recent Charlottetown Accord (one of many attempts to settle the relationship with Quebec), the National Action Committee on the Status of Women argued for 50 per cent of the seats in a reformed Senate to be guaranteed to women; when the subsequent constitutional proposals offered each province the power to decide how its senators should be elected, three out of the ten provincial premiers promised legislation to meet this demand.[1] In submissions at the same period, the Francophone Association of Alberta recommended that at least one of the six senators from each province should be drawn from that province's

---

[1] Introducing elections of any kind is a major reform, as Canadian Senators are not (at the time of writing) chosen through election.

official language minority.[2] A number of constituencies, including women, Aboriginal peoples, and Québécois, have proposed changes to the composition of the Supreme Court that would ensure their proportionate representation.[3] Various government commissions have argued that Aboriginal peoples should have the option of signing on to an Aboriginal electoral list, which would then be the basis for Aboriginal-only electoral districts;[4] and, while the Charlottetown Accord postponed the issue of Aboriginal representation in the House of Commons, it proposed that Aboriginal representation in the Senate should be guaranteed in the Constitution. Finally, if more conventionally, the less populated regions of Western and Atlantic Canada have argued that their interests are under-represented in a House of Commons that is dominated by MPs from Ontario and Quebec, and have called for a more American-style Senate to ensure equal representation for each province regardless of the density of its population. Both Senate and Supreme Court have thus become the focus for various demands for the guaranteed representation of currently under-represented groups. 'It seems likely', as Will Kymlicka notes, 'that any future proposal for Senate reform will have to address the issue of group representation, as well as regional representation.'[5]

Despite this plethora of demands for guaranteed representation

[2] W. Kymlicka, 'Group Representation in Canadian Politics', in F. L. Seidle (ed.), *Equity and Community: The Charter, Interest Advocacy and Representation* (Montreal, 1993), 63.

[3] The federal government has proposed that three (out of nine) judges should be versed in the civil law traditions of Quebec, and this proposal was reinforced by the Special Joint Committee for a Renewed Canada in its *Report of the Special Joint Committee for a Renewed Canada* (Ottawa, 1992). Women lawyers have also argued for a larger female presence, while representatives of the First Nations have argued for at least one Aboriginal judge.

[4] This was proposed by the Royal Commission on Electoral Reform and Party Financing, and seconded by the *Report of the Special Joint Committee for a Renewed Canada* in 1992. The proposals are seen mostly in relation to the Senate, rather than the House of Commons; in the words of the Special Joint Committee, the Senate 'could be, among others, a house of cultural and linguistic minorities; a house reflecting Canada's diversity, and giving special representation to women, aboriginal peoples and ethnic groups; a house of the provinces, representing provincial governments; or a house giving increased representation to the people of the smaller provinces or regions':*Report of the Special Joint Committee*, 42.

[5] W. Kymlicka, 'Three Forms of Group-Differentiated Citizenship in Canada', paper presented at a conference on 'Democracy and Difference', University of Yale, 1993, p. 6.

for disadvantaged or marginalized groups, Canadian politics is more widely known for demands for self-government or the recognition of 'distinct societies', and the unusually high level of élite concern with perceptions of political exclusion is very much driven by the fear that Quebec might secede. The main demand of the Aboriginal peoples (First Nations and Inuit, but also the Métis people, who are descended from marriages between Plains Indians and migrant French traders) has been for recognition of their inherent right of self-government, though the self-government implied in this is of a very different nature from that which has been claimed for Quebec. Some Indian bands have more than 6,000 members, but half of Canada's status Indians live in reserves with populations of less than 1,000. The considerably more numerous Métis and non-status Indians are geographically dispersed without a clear land base;[6] and self-government for these latter may mean little more than the right to run their own housing authorities or school boards. Meanwhile, other groups with no significant territorial base—women, or the many migrants from Europe, Asia, Africa, or the Caribbean who fall outside the remit of the three 'founding peoples'—have often formulated their demands for inclusion in terms of constitutional protection for sexual equality, or official recognition for multicultural diversity. The claim to equal or proportionate presence then figures just as one of many concerns.

Will Kymlicka divides Canadian demands for recognition into three broad categories. The first focuses on self-government rights; the second on multicultural rights to public support and official recognition of distinct cultural practices; and the third on those special representation rights that are more familiar from my argument so far.[7] It is tempting to regard these as different ways of dealing with

---

[6] A. C. Cairns, *Disruptions: Constitutional Struggles from the Charter to Meech Lake* (Toronto, 1991), 210–13. Status Indians are those registered as Indian, with the right to live on Indian land reserves; all these will be members of an Indian band. Non-status Indians are those (women) who have lost their status on marriage to a non-Indian; those who accepted voluntary assimilation through enfranchisement (at a time when status Indians had no right to vote); or the descendants of either of these. Métis are the descendants of marriages between Indian and French; while often regarded as just another category of non-status Indians, they have a distinct Méti identity, and have subsequently been recognized as such. See J. Ponting and R. Gibbons (eds.), *Out of Irrelevance: A Socio-Political Introduction to Indian Affairs in Canada* (Toronto, 1980), xiv.

[7] W. Kymlicka, *Multicultural Citizenship: A Liberal Theory of Minority Rights* (Oxford, 1995), ch. 2.

the same kind of problem, for in each instance some group is declaring that existing conventions of citizenship have denied them full and equal recognition. Their voices are not being heard; their particular needs and concerns are being ignored or stamped on; though formally equal, they do not enjoy equal powers. But the different responses to this seemingly common condition do not mesh neatly together. Most obviously, as Kymlicka argues, the pursuit of self-government 'seems to entail that the group should have *reduced* influence (at least on certain issues) at the federal level'.[8] If Quebec, for example, is to claim exemption from federal legislation, it hardly seems fair that MPs from Quebec should have the power to influence federal laws for the other provinces. If Aboriginal band councils are to claim autonomy over criminal justice or education in their areas, it hardly seems fair for Aboriginal MPs also to influence the nature of the provision elsewhere. The case for special representation rights then seems not so much additional as alternative to demands for local or regional autonomy.

While many of the concerns that have been expressed in Canadian politics can be formulated in the language of inclusion and exclusion, this promises a closer alliance between them than is in reality the case. All the groups so far indicated have some basis for describing themselves as excluded from the dominant consensus, and, as long as their demands are perceived in this framework, consistency suggests that any group putting forward one kind of claim should sympathize with the claims of another. This, indeed, was the rhetorical strategy adopted by the Joint Committee of the Canadian House of Commons and Senate when it delivered its *Report of the Special Joint Committee on a Renewed Canada* in early 1992. The challenge facing Canada was a fourfold 'challenge of inclusion': the first of these was 'to ensure that Quebec feels itself a full and willing partner in the constitutional family again'; the second, to include the Aboriginal peoples 'as equal partners' in the Canadian nation; the third, to meet the grievances of Western and Atlantic Canada, whose citizens had long felt themselves under-represented in an electoral system that favoured the more densely populated regions; and the fourth, to 'reflect more adequately than at present the gender balance and genuine diversity of Canadian society'.[9] In this valiant act

---

[8] Kymlicka, 'Group Representation', 73.
[9] *Report of the Special Joint Committee*, xiv–xv.

of redescription, the Joint Committee rearranged what had previously been perceived as conflicting demands along a continuum of related concerns. The upbeat style of the Report ('[t]he Canadian way is the path of gradualism, flexibility and liberty';[10] Canada is 'a rich tapestry of linguistic and cultural communities that thrive together, both nourishing and sharing their identities';[11] Canada has developed 'distinctive notions of civility, community, solidarity, and ordered liberty that transcend language and religion and set us apart from the rest of the continent'[12]) suggested that Canadians had already made the appropriate adjustments. Later events hardly justified this view. The Joint Committee had been set up to consider the most recent of many federal proposals for resolving constitutional tensions in Canada, an earlier version of which (the Meech Lake Accord) had failed to win the necessary ratification by all ten provinces. But when the revised version—the Charlottetown Accord—was subsequently put to national referendum, it was voted down by a majority in Quebec, a majority in the English-speaking provinces, and a majority among the Aboriginal peoples.

What the Committee described as different dimensions to a common challenge had been more typically viewed as contradictory through much of the 1980s, and these contradictions were relatively close to the surface even in its own recommendations. The proposals discussed for meeting the first inclusion, for example, were significantly at odds with those for meeting the fourth. The only recommendation in respect of gender parity and cultural diversity (which were clearly regarded as a lesser priority) was for a reformed Senate, whose members would be elected from multi-member constituencies by a system of proportional representation. This was presented as an enabling mechanism that would encourage political parties to draw up a more balanced slate of candidates, and thereby increase the representation of women as well as the diversity of Canada's ethnic groups. From the mid-1980s onwards, however, federal proposals for accommodating Quebec had usually included some form of provincial veto over future constitutional change, and the Committee explored the latest of these, which would have required unanimous agreement by all ten provinces on any changes to the powers, composition, and method of selection for the

---

[10] *Report of the Special Joint Committee*, 8.   [11] Ibid. 22.   [12] Ibid. 7.

Commons, Senate, or Supreme Court. Though the Committee reached no clear recommendation on this, it failed to make the obvious point that a requirement for provincial unanimity makes Senate reform far less likely.[13] If a provincial veto is the necessary price for Quebec's reinsertion into the happy family, this can obstruct other moves towards political inclusion.

I

The importance of the Canadian example lies in the limits it suggests to an exclusive politics of presence, as well as the conflicts it exposes between different strategies for dealing with the concerns of minority or disadvantaged groups. The politics of presence is in one sense at odds with conventions of liberal equality, for, when it seeks guarantees of political office to certain categories of people (and not others), it goes against the classically liberal principle that requires all citizens to have the same civil and political rights. In another sense, of course, it is merely an extension of this basic idea. If no one is to be excluded by virtue of gender, ethnicity, or language, and no one group is to be privileged over another, then certain guarantees have to be set in place to ensure that the politics is indeed evenhanded. The 'reverse discrimination' of quotas or protected constituencies aims only to rectify a previous imbalance: it does not, of itself, give differential weight to different groups. The politics of presence can then be viewed as a strategy for even stricter (but still liberal) equality, one now guaranteed by institutions, and no longer abandoned to the accidents of political life.

As the discussion of minority representation in the USA already indicates, this strategy may not be enough to deliver fair treatment of numerical minorities. It is even more evidently wanting when we turn to those perceptions of political 'exclusion' which are more appropriately designated as perceptions of political dominance or fears of incorporation into a majority norm. When Pierre Trudeau released his government's White Paper on Indian Policy in 1969, for example, he saw himself as righting historical wrongs by dismantling the century-old land reserve system and assimilating Indians into

---

[13] In the successful opposition to the Meech Lake Accord, which also proposed a provincial veto over constitutional amendments, one of the main arguments had been that this would constrain future Senate reform.

full and equal citizenship. From his perspective, this was the necessary next step from the belated enfranchisement (in 1960) of status
Indians, and the proposal 'was immediately applauded by the media,
even by opposition parties, as a triumph for liberal justice'.[14] But
what Trudeau saw as inclusion was regarded by its recipients as
forced integration, and the policy was withdrawn six months later, in
the face of bitter and almost unanimous Indian opposition. The reaction would hardly have been any different had the proposals also
included strong guarantees of Aboriginal representation in the
Canadian House of Commons and Senate; for, while earlier moves
towards special representation rights might have produced a more
mixed response, these rights do not meet the anxieties over assimilation. Canadian Indians 'do not want merely a European–Western
model of government that is run by Indians: rather, they want an
Indian government that operates in accordance with traditional principles and customs, one that rests on a spiritual base and emphasizes
group, not individual, rights'.[15] Twenty years on from the enfranchisement of status Indians, there was still 'no consensus among them
as to the wisdom of using their federal and provincial voting
rights',[16] and, while Aboriginal peoples are now pursuing a higher
profile and more adequate presence in the deliberating chambers of
the House of Commons and the Senate, this still takes second place
behind demands for Aboriginal self-government. The politics of
presence is essentially a matter of equal inclusion in the larger political unit, and this hardly deals with the aspirations of those who are
seeking to sustain their right to be different.

The politics of presence looks equally inadequate to the relationship between Quebec and the rest of Canada, where what is at issue
is the recognition of Quebec as a 'distinct society' or nation, with the
power to preserve and promote its distinctively French language,
culture, and civil law. Quebec is no longer the poor partner in economic terms: from the 1960s onwards, the expansion of the public
sector combined with innovative schemes for local development to
reverse the anglophone dominance of Quebec's economy, in terms of
ownership as well as employment. Nor is Quebec disadvantaged in

[14] W. Kymlicka, *Liberalism, Community, and Culture* (Oxford, 1989), 144.
[15] L. Little Bear, M. Bolt, and A. J. Long (eds.), *Pathways to Self-Determination:
Canadian Indians and the Canadian State* (Toronto, 1984), xvi.
[16] Ibid. xvii.

terms of its representation at federal level: if there *is* still a problem of under-representation for French-speaking Canadians, this arises only for the French-speaking minorities that live in the English-speaking provinces. Earlier patterns of disadvantage and discrimination have been successfully erased, but Quebec remains a small enclave of French language and culture in a continent where English is by far the dominant means of communication. The Official Languages Act of 1969 established the right to publicly funded education in either of the two official languages, as well as the right to deal with public bodies in either English or French. But bilingualism works best when it regulates relationships between communities that are relatively stable in numbers and power. Once this stability is disrupted, the seemingly even-handed recognition of two official languages can accelerate the dominance of one.

The startling decline in Quebec's birth rate (from one of the highest in the Western industrialized world in the late 1950s to one of the lowest today[17]) contributed to a parallel decline in the number of French speakers, and, after many decades in which francophones had made up 30 per cent of the total Canadian population, they dropped back to slightly less than a quarter. This movement coincided with an increased number of new citizens who spoke neither French nor English as their first language, and whose prospects of employment and mobility were far more likely to improve if they adopted English as their new language. Montreal, in consequence, seemed to be becoming a predominantly English-language city, and while the threat to the French language was undoubtedly exaggerated in the flow of political debate, there were legitimate grounds for concern. Fifteen years on from the controversial Loi 101 that made French the only official language in Quebec, and by far the most favoured language at work, Simon Langlois noted that English was still widely spoken in the province, and that Montreal was practically a bilingual city.[18]

[17] S. Langlois, J.-P. Baillargeon, G. Caldwell, G. Frechet, M. Gauthier, and J.-P. Simard, *Recent Social Trends in Quebec 1960–90* (Montreal, 1992), 102. Considering the Catholic Church's official position on contraception and abortion, it is rather striking that Quebec now sits with other Catholic countries, like Italy and Spain, at the bottom of the list. See also H. J. Maroney, ' "Who Has the Baby?" Nationalism, Pronatalism and the Construction of a "Demographic Crisis" in Quebec, 1960–1988', *Studies in Political Economy*, 39 (1992).

[18] He compares this to the situation in the rest of (English-speaking) Canada,

When the Parti Québécois introduced its language legislation in 1977,[19] it was still thinking in terms of a paradigm of economic disadvantage; indeed, in preliminary discussions the party explored the alternative of introducing quotas for French-speaking employees and other kinds of affirmative action at work.[20] The emphasis soon shifted to the kind of powers and autonomies that are necessary to sustain a separate and distinct identity, and this seems to move it beyond the remit of equal or proportionate presence. The problem is not that French-speaking Canadians are under-represented at work or in politics, but that, as a minority culture in a predominantly English-speaking nation, they feel their identity threatened by forces that will assimilate them into a pan-Canadian norm. They have then looked to policies that will sustain their minority language and culture, and these have included setting strict limits to the public provision of English-language education, as well as the controversial requirement for commercial signage to be exclusively in French.

Because the politics of presence always invokes some notion of proportionality between constituent groups, it already presumes a heterogeneous society—and this presumption can be precisely what some people will want to contest. In the context of Quebec, for example, the politics of presence suggests guaranteed representation for both francophones and anglophones, distributed in proportion to their numbers in the province. This would, in a sense, already pre-empt the possibility of defining Quebec as a distinct French-speaking society, for, even if the representatives from the linguistic minority were regularly outvoted on matters relating to the preservation of French language and culture, the recognition of their right

where French has all the protection of being an official language, but 'French institutions are absent, anemic, or marginalized': Langlois *et al.*, *Recent Social Trends*, 594.

[19] Where the Official Languages Act had established the rights of all individuals to deal with public bodies in either French or English, Quebec's language law limited this to a right to use either language in court; and where the federal policy of bilingualism had guaranteed the right to public education in either language, Loi 101 limited the right to publicly funded English language education to the children of English-speaking households already resident in Quebec at the time of the legislation. The legislation also required firms employing over 50 workers to embark on a francization programme which would establish French as the dominant language at work, and required commercial signage to be exclusively in French.

[20] G. Fraser, *PQ: Rene Levesque and the Parti Québécois in Power* (Toronto, 1984), 99.

to be there would have defined the province as an essentially bilingual entity. But French-speaking Québécois have not, on the whole, seen their problems as resolved through the recognition of a bilingual and bicultural Canada, and their preferred alternative is a *territorial* bilingualism, which recognizes French as the official language in one territory and English as the official language elsewhere. Nor have they welcomed the 1971 statement of policy on multiculturalism, which was designed to meet the complaints of the growing number of Canadians who are of neither French nor English extraction, and who felt their own cultural identities were being rendered invisible by the assertion of 'two Canadas'. For many Québécois, this was even worse than the original policy. In Simon Langlois's curt summary, 'French Québécois do not accept definition of their identity as one among many ethnic identities in Canada, nor do they accept the reduction of their language to the status of an ethnic language within the Canadian mosaic.'[21]

Drawing attention to the distinction between self-government and special representation rights, Will Kymlicka has argued that a clearer understanding of the difference should help dissipate some of the anxieties that are aroused by a politics of presence. When groups call for guaranteed or proportionate representation, they are politicizing their differences only to ensure their better inclusion; far from promoting a separatist politics which could threaten social cohesion, they are actively pursuing 'full membership in the larger society'.[22] When groups call for self-government rights, by contrast, they do 'pose a threat to social unity',[23] for they are always querying the authority of the larger society, and this sometimes ends up in demands for complete secession. Kymlicka's point is not that the first must be accommodated and the second resisted, but that the elision of the two seriously misrepresents what is at issue in demands for equal or proportionate presence. Self-government rights may indeed raise the spectre of future balkanization; calls for guaranteed representation are very evidently driven by the desire for fuller inclusion.

The distinction goes some way to dislodging opposition to guaranteed presence, but it also highlights the potential incompatibility between the two kinds of demand. One might well want to argue

---

[21] In Langlois *et al.*, *Recent Social Trends*, 592.
[22] Kymlicka, *Multicultural Citizenship*, 192.   [23] Ibid.

that the two *are* incompatible, and that democracies will just have to choose between the pluralistic power-sharing that is implied in a politics of presence and the preservation of ethnic or religious or linguistic homogeneity that is so often implicit in self-government rights. The fact that a significant number of people are strongly attached to each of these options is not in itself decisive. It may present us with pragmatic reasons for accommodating both kinds of concerns, but it does not establish their equal validity. Why not just take a stand on the egalitarian premiss that power should be shared between different groups? Why waste even a moment's energy on those who want to insulate themselves from difference?

This robust dimissal has its attractions, but it all too evidently cuts across one of the principles of a politics of presence. Part of the impetus behind any strategy of equal or proportionate presence is the perception that dominant groups have defined for themselves the terrain of exclusive alternatives, and that in this process they have marginalized the preoccupations of other social groups. It hardly seems legitimate then to exclude from consideration any awkward or ill-fitting concerns. If people employ their new-found voice to say they do not want to be part of my pattern—if they insist, for example, that maintaining their cultural or linguistic identity matters more to them than proportionate seats in a federal assembly, or that what they want more than anything else is the right to be left alone— I cannot consistently rule this out. To this extent, the rhetorical unity conveyed in that fourfold 'challenge of inclusion' *is* appropriate, for anyone who worries about the under-representation of women or people from ethnic minorities should equally well worry about the cultural assimilationism that can threaten distinct, minority, communities. The strategies suggested by one set of problems, however, can come into sharp conflict with the strategies suggested by the other, at which point the surface similarity begins to dissolve. Recent Canadian politics is full of examples of precisely this kind of tension, many of which coalesced around the introduction of the 1982 Charter of Rights and Freedom. The point I stress in exploring these tensions is that political presence remains a vital necessity even in the context of self-government rights.

II

Québécois nationalism evolved rapidly from the economic grievances of the 1960s to the claims for special status in the 1970s and
1980s, and, although proposals for 'sovereignty-association' were
defeated in the 1980 referendum, the Parti Québécois retained and
increased its government majority in the following year. Against this
background, the government of Quebec effectively opted out of initiatives in the rest of Canada to establish a new basis of citizenship.
In particular, it refused to sign the 1982 Constitution Act, not
because this unilaterally established Canadian control over the constitution (Quebec is no great defender of British rule), but because it
did so without resolving the status of French-speaking Canada. To
put it more strongly (and this was how it was widely perceived in
Quebec), it resolved the tensions between anglophone and francophone Canada by a settlement that marginalized the latter.

The 1982 Act included as its cornerstone a Charter of Rights and
Freedoms which many commentators have described as a consciously nation-building project—one that would, in Alan Cairns's
words, 'induce provincial residents to view and judge their government through the standardized lens of Canadian citizenship rather
than through the more variable lens of provincial residence'.[24] For
many Canadians outside Quebec, the Charter then became a mobilizing ground for new demands for political inclusion; for many
Canadians inside Quebec, it was seen as a vehicle for imposing pan-
Canadian values and identity. The rights-bearing citizen of the 1982
Charter (who bears, among other things, the right to have her children educated in the minority official language of her province) can,
from this perspective, be considered almost deliberate provocation.

One concession to Quebec was a provision that delayed implementation of the minority language rights clause until this was
agreed by the Quebec assembly. Another was the last-minute inclusion of a 'Notwithstanding clause', which enabled provincial legislatures to override major sections of the Charter for renewable
periods of five years. Quebec immediately availed itself of this

---

[24] A. C. Cairns, *Charter versus Federalism: The Dilemmas of Constitutional
Reform* (Montreal, 1992), 51. For a similar reading of the Charter—though a dif-
ferent judgement on the project—see C. Taylor, 'Shared and Divergent Values', in
R. L. Watts and D. M. Brown (eds.), *Options for a New Canada* (Toronto, 1991).

provision, but even the blanket override that the government adopted was not enough to save all Quebec's preferred laws. In a series of cases taken up under the remit of the Charter, a number of major statutes—considerably more than in any other province—were struck down as unconstitutional. Whatever the intentions of the federal government (and these had never included a desire to strengthen separatist feeling inside Quebec), the introduction of the Charter significantly heightened tensions between the province and the rest of Canada. Many Québécois came to see themselves as 'betrayed' by the rest of the country, while many Canadians outside Quebec came to see the insistence on linguistic and cultural distinctiveness as denying the rights and freedoms guaranteed in the Charter.

In similar vein, Aboriginal peoples argued that the Charter failed to give explicit recognition to their status as First Nations, and that, pending a full recognition of their inherent rights of self-government, the Charter unilaterally asserted the authority of federal government. The Charter had been introduced without the official involvement and consent of the Aboriginal peoples, and, while it gave new recognition to their treaty rights, it did this in the context of constitutionally guaranteed individual rights that could be deployed against Aboriginal self-government. Many of the representatives of Aboriginal people—like many of the representatives of French-speaking Québécois—then argued that it was up to them to formulate an appropriate Charter of Rights and Freedoms, and not a matter to be imposed from on high.

One reading of these developments suggests a deepening divide between liberal assertions of individual rights (to be established and protected through the courts) and communitarian assertions of collective goods (to be protected by government action): a real-world instantiation of what political theorists have debated as the opposition between liberal and communitarian thought. The speeches and writings of Pierre Trudeau give considerable support to such a reading, for Trudeau recurrently insisted that 'only the individual is the possessor of rights',[25] and that the central point of a constitutional charter is precisely to guarantee the inalienable rights of individuals against the collectivities that might otherwise threaten them. He

[25] P. E. Trudeau, 'The Values of a Just Society', in T. S. Axworthy and P. E. Trudeau (eds.), *Towards a Just Society: The Trudeau Years* (Ontario, 1990), 364.

recognized that individuals may gather together in 'ethnic, linguistic, religious, professional, political or other collectivities',[26] and that these individuals may then want to delegate to collectivities the task of promoting what they come to see as collective goals. But Trudeau remained very cagey over the possibility of collective rights.[27] His own formation in a Quebec ruled by 'a reactionary and authoritarian government' and 'a theocratic and obscurantist clergy'[28] left him with an abiding commitment to the freedoms of the individual, over and against any claims of ethnicity, geography, or religion. And, while he subsequently modified his liberal individualism to embrace a more multicultural pluralism, it is clear enough from his writings that he valued multiple heterogeneities primarily as a counterweight to stifling homogeneities.[29]

An alternative, and perhaps equally plausible, reading regards the 1982 Charter as enabling a new politics of assertively identity-based groups, for, while the rights proclaimed resided in individuals, the Charter also gave explicit recognition to an extensive range of disadvantaged and excluded groups. The general equality clause (section 15) was rewritten after considerable feminist pressure to make clear that equality means more than just the absence of overt discrimination;[30] while, in further specifying the right to equality regardless of 'race, national or ethnic origin, colour, religion, sex, age or mental or physical disability', the Charter gave new visibility to what Alan Cairns dubs 'section 15 equality-seekers'.[31] Other clauses reaffirmed Canada's status as a multicultural country, noted the rights of official language minorities, asserted that none of the provisions should be read as overriding the as yet unsettled rights of Aboriginals, gave the first constitutional recognition to the Métis as part of the

[26] Ibid. Note how the inclusion of 'professional' and 'political' collectivities turns this into a relatively anodyne list of pressure groups.

[27] Trudeau allows, in certain unspecified instances, for 'some collective rights of minorities', (Trudeau, 'Values', 364), but more typically he stresses the way that so-called minority rights are in truth the rights of individual members within minorities.

[28] Ibid. 358.

[29] R. Cook, '"I Never Thought I Could Be so Proud" . . . The Trudeau–Levesque Debate', in Axworthy and Trudeau, *Towards a Just Society*, 353.

[30] As finally formulated, every individual 'is equal before the law and under the law and has the right to the equal benefit and protection of the law'.

[31] A. C. Cairns, 'Constitutional Change and the Three Equalities', in R. L. Watts and D. M. Brown (eds.), *Options For a New Canada* (Toronto, 1991), 84.

Aboriginal peoples, and made a strong statement guaranteeing the Charter's rights and freedoms equally to women and men. The result, as Cairns sees it, was 'a Janus-faced document, presenting both liberal individualism and a constitutionalization of the linguistic, ethnic, racial, cultural and sex identities of Canadians'.[32] Though formulated predominantly in terms of individual rights, the Charter also confirmed perceptions of Canada as a complex heterogeneity of differently treated *groups*. To this extent, it fundamentally changed the nature of political action and the roll-call of political actors.

The change should not be exaggerated, for the results of the Charter have been more mixed than its supporters must have hoped. In relation to women's equality, a number of cases financed by the Women's Legal Action Fund successfully established sexual harassment and discrimination against pregnant women as illegitimate forms of sexual discrimination. But, in the face of a virtual 'epidemic of cases brought by men' (including the famous case where the so-called 'rape shield' which protected rape victims from cross-examination on their sexual history was declared unconstitutional), 'proactive quickly turned to reactive'.[33] Feminist lawyers found themselves having to fend off what they saw as abuses of the Charter to strike down protections for women—cases, for example, where maternity provision was claimed as unequal (because differential) treatment, or where abortion was said to deny the constitutionally guaranteed right to life. The point Cairns makes is that, quite apart from the specific gains or losses to particular constituencies, the Charter provided a symbolic focus for new demands for political inclusion.

This was to become very apparent in the course of 1987 and 1988, when one of many initiatives was launched that would, in Prime Minister Mulroney's words, 'welcome Quebec back to the Canadian constitutional family'.[34] As with the later Charlottetown Accord, the Meech Lake Accord proposed to recognize Quebec as a distinct society within Canada; it also offered all provinces a range of additional powers, including a constitutional veto, the right to opt out of

[32] Cairns, *Charter versus Federalism*, 79.
[33] S. Razack, *Canadian Feminism and the Law: The Women's Legal Education and Action Fund and the Pursuit of Equality* (Toronto, 1991), 62.
[34] Quoted in R. M. Campbell and L. A. Pal, *The Real World of Canadian Politics* (Ontario, 1991), 91.

certain federal spending programmes, and the right to negotiate immigration policies tailored to the needs of each province. As cynics might have predicted, these latter were warmly welcomed by the provincial prime ministers, and, initially at least, the proposals were supported by one in two Canadians.[35]

Despite this, the Accord rapidly became the focus of wide-ranging opposition. A formidable array of individuals and groups testified to the Special Joint Committee of the Senate and House of Commons in 1987 and the Manitoba Task Force on Meech Lake in 1988, nearly all of them criticizing the proposals. Objections ranged from fears that the distinct society clause would be used to reduce the rights of women and linguistic minorities, through complaints that the demands of Aboriginal groups were being sidelined by the exclusive preoccupation with Quebec, to concerns that the constitutional veto would block the chances of either Senate reform or the upgrading of territories into provinces. Underlying all this variety was a perception that the Meech Lake proposals sacrificed the concerns of certain groups to the demands of others. Focusing primarily on a resolution that would be acceptable to Quebec, the proposals seemed to back away from the more multiple inclusions of the Charter.

In a particularly evocative account of some of the group and individual representations, Alan Cairns describes a deeply felt sense of political marginality and exclusion:

The representatives of women's groups, of aboriginals, or visible minorities, of supporters of multiculturalism, along with northerners and basic defenders of the Charter, employ the vocabulary of personal and group identity, of being included or excluded, of being treated with respect as a worthy participant or being cast into the audience as a spectator as one's fate is being decided by others. They employ the language of status—they are insulted, wounded, hurt, offended, bypassed, not invited, ignored, left out, and shunted aside. They evaluate their treatment through the lens of pride, dignity, honour, propriety, legitimacy, and recogition—or their reverse. Their discourse is a minority, outsider discourse.They clearly distrust established governing elites. They are in, but not of, the constitution. They are apprehensive parvenus. [36]

---

[35] Ibid. 99. This had dropped to one in four by April 1988.
[36] Cairns, *Disruptions*, 132.

This discourse of exclusion and inclusion did not take the form of any very specific demands for political presence. Most group representatives dealt more generally in calls for wider consultation and fuller recognition of previously ignored perspectives and concerns, and they repeatedly complained of decisions being taken over their heads. The Meech Lake Accord had been put together by a cabal of eleven First Ministers (all, of course, white, middle-class, men) and presented to provincial legislatures for unamended ratification. On Cairns's reading of the subsequent reaction, the Charter had given a new recognition and legitimacy to citizen action, and this was being blatantly overruled in both the content and process of the Accord. By June 1990, the proposals had failed to meet the required deadline for ratification. They were finally and symbolically killed off in the Manitoba legislature, where Elijah Harper (working with the Assembly of Manitoba Chiefs) refused the unanimous consent that would have permitted ratification. Two years later, a similar set of proposals was defeated in national referendum.

III

The 1980s metaphor of the 'rainbow coalition' suggests an optimistic scenario in which those groups excluded from the dominant consensus—women, blacks, gays and lesbians, the disabled, the non-unionized, the poor—can unite in common cause against the complacencies of those in power. The more uncomfortable reality is that different bases of marginality or exclusion can generate conflict between different groups. In the Canadian context, concessions designed to meet Quebec's concerns for linguistic and cultural autonomy were perceived as threatening the interests and concerns of a multiplicity of other individuals and groups; while developments that gave legitimacy to these individuals and groups were perceived as threatening the integrity of Quebec. In a recent discussion of these tensions, Charles Taylor argues that contemporary Canada contains within it two seemingly divergent forms of national identity.[37] Québécois identity is sustained by its linguistic and cultural distinctiveness as a society of French-speaking Canadians, while the identity of Canada-outside-Quebec (COQ) is secured primarily through its sense of distinctiveness from the USA.

[37] Taylor, 'Shared and Divergent Values'.

Key elements in the latter, Taylor argues, include the sense of pride in living in a less violent and conflict-ridden society, and the commitment to more generous and inclusive forms of social provision, as through the Canadian health service; major new elements include the commitment to multiculturalism and the principles of the 1982 Charter. But from Quebec's perspective, multiculturalism seems to downgrade the importance of the French 'fact' in Canada, while the individualism that underwrites the Charter encourages the view that a pursuit of strong collective goals is potentially, if not intrinsically, illiberal. 'COQ's new found Charter patriotism is making it less capable of acknowledging the legitimacy of collective goals';[38] but what is at issue here, Taylor argues, is not really liberalism and its alternatives. The real question is whether diversity can be accommodated only by withdrawing from substantive commitments (thus through a broadly procedural liberalism), or whether a deeper diversity can be tolerated which allows for the desire to sustain a specific (in this case French) identity.

Liberalism need not be defined by neutrality, nor by an unchanging list of individual rights which always and everywhere trump collective goals. Some rights are more fundamental than others; the right to free speech, Taylor argues, is surely more fundamental than the right to commercial signage in the language of one's choice.[39] What keeps a society liberal is not that it retreats from any pronouncements on what constitutes the good life, but that, in pursuing its own conception of the good, it none the less respects those who disagree. 'A society with strong collective goals can be liberal, on this view, provided it is also capable of respecting diversity, especially when it concerns those who do not share its goals; and provided it can offer adequate safeguards for fundamental rights.'[40]

The question then is what counts as adequate safeguards. Though every national women's group in Canada stated its support for Quebec's claim to be recognized as a distinct society,[41] women's groups outside (and to some extent, also inside) Quebec took the

---

[38] Ibid. 66.

[39] There is 'something exaggerated, a dangerous overlooking of an essential boundary, in speaking of fundamental rights to things like commercial signage in the language of one's choice' (Taylor, 'Shared and Divergent Values', 71).

[40] Ibid.

[41] L. Smith, 'Could the Meech Lake Accord Affect the Protection of Equality Rights for Women and Minorities in Canada?', *Constitutional Forum*, 1 (1990), 18.

refusal to sign the Charter as a worrying indication that women's equality would not be guaranteed. What, asked Lynn Smith, if Quebec's Code Civile proved to be less advantageous to women in its division of property on divorce: would a Quebec women be able to appeal to the general equality provisions in the Charter, or would these be overruled by the civil law traditions of Quebec?[42] Or what, as various women's groups asked in their submissions on the Meech Lake Accord, if greater autonomy for Quebec enabled its government to restrict contraception and abortion in order to stem the falling birth rate? Taylor describes such fears as 'silliness',[43] but, in the light of the pro-natalist pronouncements which have periodically surfaced in Quebec,[44] they were not as silly as he claims. The anxieties were exaggerated, but what made them inappropriate was not so much the intrinsic liberalism of French-Canadian identity, nor any constitutional guarantees that secured gender equality; it was the prominence and vigour of Québécois feminism that made a nonsense of these fears. The main safeguard, that is, lay in a powerfully egalitarian feminism, which affected all of Quebec's political parties, but proved to be particularly influential inside the Parti Québécois (PQ). It was political presence, rather than the law, that provided the surest protection.

Where other radical forces seemed to adopt a self-denying ordinance on the election (in 1976) of a reforming and social democratic PQ government, feminists kept up and increased their pressure; in the words of one commentator, 'the women's movement was virtually the only pressure group that had not, in some way, folded up its tent'.[45] Abortion was one major mobilizing issue here. In Canada (as in the USA), the availability of abortion has been established through judicial decision rather than legislative majorities, and the role of each province in agreeing to fund abortion has been decisive in making abortion more freely available. Despite the historic power of the Catholic Church in Quebec, the Parti Québécois took the lead in announcing that it would not prosecute doctors performing abortions, and later followed this with provision for public funding.

[42] L. Smith, 'Could the Meech Lake Accord Affect the Protection of Equality Rights for Women and Minorities in Canada?', *Constitutional Forum*, 1 (1990), 18–19.

[43] Taylor, 'Shared and Divergent Values', 68.

[44] Maroney, ' "Who Has the Baby?" '   [45] Fraser, *PQ*, 120.

Much of this was the result of feminist activism, as evidenced in the overwhelming vote at the 1977 party convention (against the fierce opposition of the party leader) in favour of decriminalizing abortion and establishing the 'right to motherhood by free consent'.[46] By the end of the 1980s, when it was still impossible to win a majority in the Canadian House of Commons for legalizing abortion, and when several provinces had started to impose severe restrictions on when and where abortions could be carried out, it was the governments of Quebec and Ontario (the other province most marked by feminist activity) that came closest to allowing women the power to decide, and that were the most generous in covering the costs.[47]

Political presence—not in this case guaranteed, but sustained through political activity—proved to be the main safeguard for women's equality. But 'the articulation of feminism and optimistic nationalism was fragile',[48] and particularly so when feminists found themselves landed with the blame for the loss of the 1980 referendum. Lise Payette, the first woman in the Parti Québécois cabinet, and its first Minister for the Status of Women, had made a speech attacking the Liberal Party leader as someone who wanted a Quebec full of Yvettes (a reference to the conventionally docile domesticity of a character in primary school reading texts); 'blunder of blunders', as she later called it,[49] she went on to say that he was even married to an Yvette. The subsequent mobilization of self-proclaimed Yvettes was orchestrated by Liberal Party members and women active in the 'No' campaign, and proved one of the turning points in the campaign against 'sovereignty-association'. Feminists were later marginalized in the pro-natalism of the mid- to late 1980s, when exaggerated fears of a demographic crisis encouraged political parties to pursue family policies that would raise the birth rate.[50]

---

[46] Ibid. 119.

[47] In Canada, as in the USA, it has been legal judgments—followed by government decisions over funding—that have opened up or closed down facilities for abortion. In 1989, the fears of federal charter activists were partially confirmed when the Quebec Courts interpreted the Quebec Charter of Rights and Freedoms as recognizing foetal rights to life. This judgment was then overturned by the Supreme Court. For an overview of abortion politics in Canada, see Campbell and Pal, *Real World of Canadian Politics*, ch. 1.

[48] Maroney, ' "Who Has the Baby?" ', 15.   [49] Fraser, *PQ*, 222.

[50] Heather Jon Maroney argues that feminists were wrong-footed by these later developments, because they had earlier tried to co-opt nationalist birth anxieties to press the importance of better maternity leave or child care. '[T]his discursive move

IV

Despite this worrying development, the complex interplay between nationalism and feminism in Quebec warns against any easy assumption that those pursuing cultural identity and autonomy must be less bothered about gender equality; to this extent, at least, it reinforces Charles Taylor's point that caring about one's culture does not necessarily make one illiberal. But it also reinforces my own arguments about the importance of political presence, for it was the vigorous representation of what might otherwise have been marginalized voices that kept gender equality on the political agenda. Much the same point can be made about the relationship between self-government and gender equality in the politics of Aboriginal communities. Here, too, considerations of equality have often threatened to become a casualty of equally pressing demands for self-government, and here, too, it was the campaigning efforts of women who refused to let themselves be marginalized that achieved a more amicable resolution.

One major example of this arose from the unequal treatment of Indian women and men that was enshrined in the original Indian Act. When the Act was introduced, it imposed a European understanding of patrilineal descent, subsuming wives under their husbands. Indian men who married non-Indian women then retained their status as Indians, and could pass this on to their children; but Indian women who married non-Indian men lost their status, and hence their right to live on reservation land. This reformulation of gender relations did not go unchallenged by Indian leaders; indeed, the General Council of Ontario and Quebec Indians sought an amendment in 1872, arguing that 'Indian women may have the privilege of marrying when and whom they please without subjecting themselves to exclusion or expulsion from the tribe.'[51] The provision was none the less passed, thereby introducing into Indian society the norms and presumptions of a patriarchal Europe.

A later challenge under the 1960 Bill of Rights was set aside on the

left unchallenged the charge that feminism itself was responsible for falling birth rates', (Maroney, ' "Who Has the Baby?" ', 27), and as demographic pro-natalism became more prominent in government policy feminists were thrown on the defensive.

[51] Ponting and Gibbons, *Out of Irrelevance*, 5–6.

spurious procedural ground that a law that applied equally to all Indian women could not be viewed as discriminatory, and the 1970 Report of the Royal Commission on the Status of Women then recommended legislative amendment to equalize the rights of Indian men and women. In the course of the 1970s and 1980s, however, leaders of the First Nations argued that this should take second place behind the as yet unresolved demands for Aboriginal self-government. What was at issue here was whether the federal government had the right to decide on this matter. The Council of Six Nations, for example, argued that it was not for the federal government to determine who was or was not to be deemed an Indian, and it resisted what it saw as an intrusion on its own rights to self-determination. The resulting impasse was part of what led to the breakdown of the Second Constitutional Conference on Aboriginal Rights in 1984, after which the Assembly of First Nations ran half-page advertisements in a number of major newspapers, arguing that this was not an issue of sexual equality or inequality, but of 'the right of individual First Nations to determine their own citizenship, the preservation of their cultural identities and the right to exercise self-government'.[52]

The arguments against change were as much about practicalities as about principle; First Nations leaders were concerned that equalization might give immediate rights of residence on reserve land to an estimated 15,000 women and 57,000 children, and they argued that the government should contribute extra land and resources to correct what had after all been its own mistakes.[53] First Nations women, meanwhile, campaigned vigorously on the issue, successfully persuading a number of band councils to apply to the Minister for Indian Affairs for unilateral suspension of the sexually discriminatory provision.[54] The Canadian women's movement as a whole also took up the unequal treatment of women under the Indian Act as a major campaigning concern; but, given the endless scope for playing off the overwhelmingly white women's movement against

[52] F. Morton, 'Group Rights versus Individual Rights in the Charter: The Special Cases of Natives and the Québécois', in N. Nevitte and A. Kornberg (eds.), *Minorities and the Canadian State* (Ontario, 1985), 77.

[53] Ibid. 76.

[54] Little Bear *et al.*, *Pathways to Self-Determination*, 81 n.

the concerns of Aboriginal communities,[55] the interventions of First Nations women were particularly important. In 1985 the Act was finally amended, establishing formal equality between women and men.

In this case, the under-representation of women on the associations that speak on behalf of the First Nations potentially undermined moves towards sexual equality; for, even if we accept the legitimacy of some of the concerns that were raised, it is reasonable enough to assume that the Assembly of First Nations would have adopted a different stance had it been more representative of women. Certainly, organizations of Aboriginal women have been significantly more inclined to support federal interventions on sexual equality, and noticeably less willing to trust to Aboriginal self-government in such affairs. Not that Aboriginal women speak with one voice on such issues: while some have looked to the Charter of Rights and Freedoms as an important protection for women, others have referred back to Aboriginal traditions of consensus government as more conducive to gender equality.[56] But in their representation to the Special Joint Committee on a Renewed Canada, the Native Women's Association of Canada strongly supported the continued application of the federal Charter of Rights and Freedoms, at a time when other Aboriginal organizations still saw the Charter as an inappropriate imposition from outside.[57] And, in a particularly direct example of the politics of presence, the Association later

[55] During the campaign to tighten up the equality provisions of the Charter, the Canadian media repeatedly portrayed the women's lobby as indifferent to the even more pressing claims of Aboriginal peoples, despite the fact that the women's organizations had consistently supported the additional amendments being pursued by Aboriginal groups. See P. Kome, *The Taking of Twenty-Eight: Women Challenge the Constitution* (Toronto, 1983), 101.

[56] See the discussion in J. Tully, 'The Crisis of Identification: The Case of Canada', in J. Dunn (ed.), *Contemporary Crisis of the Nation State?* special issue of *Political Studies*, 42 (1994). In a fascinating account of the role of clan mothers in selecting male chiefs for the council of the Mohawk Nation, Tom Porter argues that this gives precedence to qualities rather than opinions, thus to the more community-related qualities of integrity or honesty or fairness (which clan mothers are thought to be particularly well placed to judge) rather than to the various opinions different contenders might express. It would be absurd to describe this selection of exclusively male chiefs as an exemplification of the politics of presence, but it shares some interesting common ground with the arguments that query representation by professed ideas. See T. Porter, 'Traditions of the Constitution of the Six Nations', in Little Bear *et al.*, *Pathways to Self-Determination*.

[57] *Report of the Special Joint Committee*, 31.

appealed to the Charter to challenge the under-representation of Aboriginal women in the negotiations around the Charlottetown Accord. The debacle of the Meech Lake Accord had encouraged the federal and provincial governments to set up what they saw as a far more democratic and inclusive process of negotiation to draw up the Charlottetown agreement, and representatives of four of the national Aboriginal organizations[58] were invited as participants in this. Not included, however, was the Native Women's Association of Canada, which argued that the other Aboriginal organizations were too male-dominated to protect women's rights, and waged a 'high-profile campaign of opposition to the Accord'.[59] The Federal Court of Appeal ruled that the Association's charter rights to freedom of expression had indeed been compromised, but fell short of agreeing that their exclusion infringed gender equality.[60] Significantly enough, the proposed agreement then did seem to allow for self-government rights to trump the sexual equality provisions in the Charter.[61]

Though constitutional guarantees offer one potential safeguard against policies that might sacrifice gender equality to other concerns, the strongest protection for women's equality lies in the mobilization of women to make their (various) voices heard. Protection through the courts can be an important element in this, except that what is so often at issue is what counts as a 'fundamental right'. Charles Taylor asks whether we have a fundamental right to commercial signs in our own language. Do we, by extension, have a fundamental right to abortion or equal status in marriage? Taylor distinguishes between those fundamental liberties 'that should never be infringed and therefore ought to be unassailably entrenched' and those 'privileges and immunities that are important, but that can be

---

[58] The Assembly of First Nations, the Native Council of Canada, the Inuit Tapirisat of Canada, and the Métis National Council.

[59] M. E. Turpel, 'Aboriginal People's Struggle for Fundamental Political Change', in K. McRoberts and P. A. Monahan (eds.), *The Charlottetown Accord, the Referendum, and the Future of Canada* (Toronto, 1993), 132.

[60] Mary Ellen Turpel notes that other Aboriginal women's association did not lend their support to the litigation, and that the associations that were invited to participate in the negotiations included some high profile women: see 'Aboriginal People's Struggle', 132–3.

[61] A. F. Bayefsky, 'The Effect of Aboriginal Self-Government on the Rights and Freedoms of Women', *Network Analyses: Reactions* (October 1992).

revoked or restricted for reasons of public policy'.[62] This is an entirely legitimate distinction—some things *are* more fundamental than others—but the boundary is more permeable than Taylor's account suggests. His own list of the fundamental rights of the liberal tradition—'rights to life, liberty, due process, free speech, free practice of religion'—tails off into the necessary 'and so on',[63] for it is difficult to draw up the definitive list that will stand for all future occasions. What we count as basic rights and liberties is continually rewritten by those who act on the political stage, and this reinforces the importance of 'being there' when the boundaries and distinctions are drawn.

V

The multi-layered complexity of Canada's 'challenge of inclusion' militates against any single strategy for resolving the various claims, and it exposes the limits of a politics of presence when what is at issue is the degree of self-government or provincial autonomy. 'The right to self-government', as Will Kymlicka puts it, 'is a right against the authority of the federal government, not a right to share in the exercise of that authority';[64] and Aboriginal groups, in particular, have been wary of laying claims to guaranteed representation at federal level when this might seem to concede federal authority over Aboriginal affairs. The main qualification to this has been a concern, among both Québécois and Aboriginal peoples, to ensure some proportionate representation on the Supreme Court. As Kymlicka also stresses, the right to self-government does seem to entail a right to representation on those bodies that have the power to regulate or modify the degree of self-government, and to this extent self-government is still associated with a politics of presence. But on the whole, the kind of inclusion or recognition that has been sought by Québécois and Aboriginal peoples is inclusion as a distinct, self-governing entity. The argument is about degrees of autonomy within what is claimed as a multinational state.

However, the 'nations' implied in this are not—if they ever were—homogeneous. Quebec, for example, includes eleven First Nations

---

[62] C. Taylor, 'The Politics of Recognition', in A. Gutmann (ed.), *Multiculturalism and the 'Politics of Recognition'* (Princeton, 1992), 59.

[63] Ibid.   [64] Kymlicka, 'Group Representation', 74.

within its present borders, occupying over half the territory; it also includes 800,000 anglophones, as well as a variety of others who may identify with none of the three founding peoples. If Quebec were to secede, it would still have to deal with its own internal cultural diversity.[65] Meanwhile, the Aboriginal peoples 'do not wish to return to their pre-invasion political identities, nor could they if they so wished';[66] as James Tully notes, they have drawn variously on their own traditions, Canadian law, international law, and even the Indian Act to define the forms of self-government they want to develop, and are engaged in a continuous renegotiation of their cultural and political identity. Even the politics of self-government then intermeshes with the concerns of political presence, for in these processes of negotiation it will always matter who gets a voice.

That said, Canadian politics does clarify some of the limits to a politics of presence when what is at issue is cultural dominance or forced assimilation. Demands for equal or proportionate presence arise only in the context of heterogeneity, and they draw attention to the kinds of exclusion that come into play when differences by gender or ethnicity or religion or language are ruled out of the political process. But in pursuing a strategy of proportionality, the politics of presence tends to sideline what may be equally pressing concerns about sustaining cultural or linguistic identity. This may not be intrinsically at odds with the right of differently constituted communities to retain their distinction and difference, but it does make heterogeneity a more positive value. Since heterogeneity can also be perceived as a threat (as when the official attachment to multiculturalism is said to undermine the uniqueness of French identity), this may not be sensitive enough to other perceptions of political dominance.

One might think, by extension, of the kinds of argument that have recently surfaced in Britain over the equal treatment of non-Christian minorities. When societies contain a multiplicity of different religious groups, the secular separation between Church and State looks the only way to be even-handed: no religion should be privileged over another; there should be a complete separation between religion and politics. The only difficulty with this is that secularism can generate its own intolerance, sometimes leading to

---

[65] Tully, 'The Crisis of Identification', 79–80.   [66] Ibid. 90.

insensitive treatment of those people who still care about religious practices and beliefs. It is with this in mind that Tariq Modood, for example, has argued against the disestablishment of the Anglican Church, seeing this as the project of a proselytizing secularism rather than something that would benefit the non-Christian religions. Britain, as he notes, 'is a country in which the non-religious or the passively religious form an overwhelming majority',[67] and the growing communities of non-Christian believers (Muslim, Hindu, Sikh) may then have more to fear from a triumphal secularism than from the relatively modest role currently claimed by the Anglican Church. In principle, at least, secularism looks the most appropriate strategy for any country that incorporates a multiplicity of faiths—but *radical* secularism can be very illiberal.

The argument does not, in my view, weaken the case for a secular solution, but it does serve as a reminder that it is not so easy to be even-handed. In the context of a secular society that none the less contains a diversity of religions, democracy cannot be well served by practices that privilege one church over others; but nor can it be well served by practices that privilege secular values over religious ones, or religious values over secular beliefs. Almost any way of formulating this, however, seems to put it in the framework of a secular solution—one that then diminishes the significance of religion—and the effects may then be less genuinely equal on all the relevant groups.

In the Canadian 'challenge of inclusion', the pursuit of equal or proportionate presence may look the most even-handed way of meeting the needs of all constituent groups. But the strategy tends to privilege heterogeneity over homogeneity, and power-sharing over collective goals. This cannot of itself meet the concerns of Aboriginal self-government, or the far more contested preoccupation with maintaining a 'distinct society' in Quebec. And while we could always argue that the preservation of distinct (and more homogeneous) communities is itself an illegitimate goal, this is at odds with the underlying premiss of a politics of presence, which seeks to articulate the needs and concerns of previously subordinate groups. (It is also too obviously illiberal.)

The relationship between self-government rights and equal or proportionate presence, then, remains complex, and sometimes conflictual. The conclusion is hardly surprising: that a politics of presence is not the only thing we may need in order to achieve democratic equality.

CHAPTER 6

―――

Deliberation, accountability,
and interest

The case studies explored in Chapters 3, 4, and 5 throw up a variety of potentially divergent issues, but one feature is common to all. In each instance, the politics of presence has referred back to a notion that different groups have different kinds of interest, and that, failing more equitable distribution of political office between different groups, there is little basis for believing that public policy will be equitable between all. The precise character of group interest has proved somewhat slippery; thus, interests may be gendered without any implication that all women share the same set of interests; racial and ethnic minorities may have a strong sense of themselves as a distinct social group, but this can coincide with an equally strong sense of division over policy goals; territorial minorities may see their own interests and concerns as ignored by the wider community, but still have to grapple with their internal diversity. In much of what I have argued so far, I have treated this as part of the dynamic between ideas and presence, arguing that any simplistic assertion of a unified group interest underplays the importance of policy debate. This should be understood, however, as a modification rather than an attack on group interest, and it does not, of itself, challenge the status of group interest in politics. At this point in the argument, I want to return more directly to the relationship with deliberative democracy, and what this latter tradition implies about the role of interest in politics.

The project of equal or proportionate presence moves in close but uneasy association with the project of deliberative democracy. The two converge in recognizing a problem of political exclusion, and both of them have addressed who is present in political debate. But the relationship remains distinctly touchy, partly because the first has a self-consciously reformist bias. It chooses to deal with representative democracy as currently given, and it focuses its attention on the composition of existing élites. Additional links are often forged to programmes of wider and deeper democratization; in the arguments for gender parity, for example, this further connection is frequently made. But the politics of presence distinguishes itself from the more ambitious explorations of deliberative democracy by concentrating on reforms that are immediately achievable or mechanisms that are already in place. It occupies what its own advocates may ruefully acknowledge as a half-way house of remedial reform.

Deliberative democracy, by contrast, tends to start from characterizations of the ideal. Joshua Cohen sees deliberative democracy as a 'fundamental political ideal',[1] whose independent value must first be established before moving on to consider its material conditions. The ideal then serves as a guide for the more day-to-day work around institutional design: if we know what we are aiming for, we can more readily distinguish between those conditions and structures that best encourage its development, and those that would stand in its way. In their later work on associational democracy, Cohen and Rogers then appeal to deliberative principles to determine which policies would best promote deliberative practice.[2]

This initial point of distinction is not in itself decisive, for there is no intrinsic contradiction between what could be short-term and longer-term goals. But the contrast shades into a more substantial set of problems, revolving around the different status each attaches to group interest. Though the arguments for including previously excluded groups and perspectives are rarely couched solely in terms of representing group interest, this is inevitably one part of the whole. In some cases, this becomes the dominant concern, and it then runs up against a deep distaste among deliberative democrats for the politics based around interest. From the other side, of course, deliberative democrats sometimes seem to inhabit a world of romanticized dreams, and when they invoke the supposedly common concerns that are going to transcend the politics of faction, they expose themselves to legitimate criticism about underplaying genuine conflicts of interest.

---

[1] J. Cohen, 'Deliberation and Democratic Legitimacy', in A. Hamlin and P. Pettit (eds.), *The Good Polity: Normative Analysis of the State* (Oxford, 1989), 17.

[2] J. Cohen and J. Rogers, 'Secondary Associations and Democratic Governance', *Politics and Society*, 20/4 (1992).

Though Iris Young now puts her arguments for group representation more explicitly in the context of what she prefers to call 'communicative democracy', her initial formulations in *Justice and the Politics of Difference* relied heavily on criticizing this politics of transcendence. When oppressed groups are called upon to put their own partial interests aside—to address the shared concerns of all humanity, to think beyond their own interests and needs—this injunction can lock them into the very structures they are trying to dislodge. The ideal of impartiality is always, in Young's view, 'an idealist fiction',[3] one that imagines us capable of standing apart from previous experience to reach a universal point of view. The fiction turns out to be peculiarly advantagous to those groups whose dominance is secured by long established structures of privilege. Such groups need not make their own partiality explicit: to borrow from Cass Sunstein's formulation, they can appeal to doctrines of legal neutrality to defend neutrality in relation to the status quo.[4] When oppressed groups, by contrast, challenge this alleged neutrality, 'their claims are heard as those of biased, selfish special interests'[5] that seek special treatment or differential rights.

In the wider literature, interest group pluralism has been criticized for failing to distribute political influence fairly: the power of each group is never strictly proportional to its numbers; and those who start out with more resources end up reaping maximum rewards. Interest groups backed by money have more power than those that have limited financial resources. Interest groups that are already recognized by governments (as in the tripartite corporatism once favoured by many European democracies) have more ready access to the policy-making process than those that are not yet acknowledged. Well organized interest groups have more power than those whose membership remains dispersed. Thus, consumer groups are notoriously weaker than producers, while the interests of housewives, pensioners, or the unemployed have less powerful advocates than organized business and organized labour. Since interest groups engage in rent-seeking behaviour, using their organizational or

[3] I. M. Young, *Justice and the Politics of Difference* (Princeton, 1990), 104.
[4] C. R. Sunstein, 'Neutrality in Constitutional Law (with Special Reference to Pornography, Abortion and Surrogacy)', *Columbia Law Review*, 92/1 (1992).
[5] Young, *Justice and the Politics of Difference*, 116.

financial superiority to reap even higher rewards,[6] this imbalance has serious effects; and when the power they exert is so obviously disproportional to the numbers they represent, it conflicts with most understandings of political equality.

One time-honoured solution has been to accept group interest factionalism as an inevitable part of political life, but to try to equalize the access to include previously under-represented groups. This was roughly the line James Madison took when he identified the 'mischiefs of faction', though Madison was less concerned with equalizing access than with encouraging the factions to cancel each other out. Cohen and Rogers categorize the more ambitious modern-day equivalent as an 'egalitarian pluralism',[7] and, on at least one reading of the arguments for race-conscious districting, this is what is being pursued in voting rights litigation in the USA. But increased representation for the under-represented can modify, without substantially altering, the practices of majoritarian rule; and even when it does promise a more substantial review of overall policy direction, it does this within the framework of a zero-sum game. In the politics of interest group bargaining, 'what I get must be taken from someone else'.[8] Interests that differ are perceived as in conflict; and either one wins out over the others, or all adjust to a compromise that delivers less than anyone wants. Theorists of deliberative democracy argue that something more is both possible and desirable: a transformative politics that extends the range of potential solutions.

Though 'deliberative democracy' is only a recent formulation, its central preoccupations are shared by a wide collection of theorists, some of whom have adopted an alternative name. Benjamin Barber, for example, organizes his own case for a more deliberative democracy around the contrast between strong and weak democracy;[9] John Dryzek develops his blend of critical theory and participatory democracy under the rubric of discursive democracy;[10] Cass

---

[6] J. J. Mansbridge, 'A Deliberative Theory of Interest Representation', in M. P. Pettraca (ed.), *The Politics of Interest* (Boulder, Colo., 1992).

[7] The other two strands they identify in contemporary American debate are neoliberal constitutionalism and civic republicanism; see Cohen and Rogers, 'Secondary Associations', 394.

[8] Mansbridge, 'A Deliberative Theory', 37.

[9] B. Barber, *Strong Democracy* (Berkeley, 1984).

[10] J. S. Dryzek, *Discursive Democracy: Politics, Policy and Political Science* (Cambridge, 1990).

Sunstein alternates between a language of deliberation and a language of civic republicanism.[11] Iris Marion Young prefers to describe her own version as communicative rather than deliberative democracy, not in any uncritical endorsement of Habermas's theory of communicative action, but as a way of recognizing that discussion often starts from initial incomprehension, and that 'participants in communicative interaction must reach out to one another to forestall or overcome misunderstanding'.[12] Though I take her point that deliberation may suggest an overly dispassionate kind of discussion between people who already share the same way of talking, the distinction she makes between deliberation and communication is not as important as the underlying areas of convergence.

The common core that characterizes theories of deliberative or communicative or discursive democracy is that political engagement can change initial statements of preference and interest. All combine in criticism of that interest-based democracy which sees political activity primarily in terms of instrumental rationality; which reduces the act of representation to the representation of pre-given, unchanging preference; and conceives of government as engaged in aggregation. When interest aggregation is the name of the game, this not only justifies majority rule in majority interest (if they have secured a majority, how can anyone legitimately object?) but also actively discourages a more exploratory politics which could identify new areas of common interest. No contemporary theorist thinks of 'the common good' as something that is easy to identify or define, and most accept initial formulations of preference or interest as a necessary starting point for what might later emerge. This is no simple recovery of those earlier traditions which counterposed a unified public good to the distractions of self-love or the sordid preoccupations of individual and group interest. What deliberative democracy insists on, however, is the capacity for formulating new positions in the course of discussion with others; as Jane Mansbridge puts this,

11 C. R. Sunstein, 'Beyond the Republican Revival', *Yale Law Journal*, 97/8 (1988); C. R. Sunstein, 'Preferences and Politics', *Philosophy and Public Affairs*, 20/1 (1991); C. R. Sunstein, 'Democracy and Shifting Preferences', in D. Copp, J. Hampton, and J. E. Roemer (eds.), *The Idea of Democracy* (Cambridge, 1993).
12 I. M. Young, 'Justice and Communicative Democracy', in R. Gottlieb (ed.), *Tradition, Counter-Tradition, Politics: Dimensions of Radical Philosophy* (Philadelphia, 1994), 128.

'deliberation often makes possible solutions that were impossible before the process began'.[13]

The very requirement for public argument (having to convince others to your point of view) is said to help us revise and reconsider our positions, for we become aware of consequences we had not previously considered and concerns we had previously overlooked. In the privacy and anonymity of the ballot box, we have no chance to review our own judgements against what others have to say. But in a context of fuller information and more open and public debate, we may come to see our initial preferences as based on ignorance or prejudice—and, once we see them in this light, these preferences are already undergoing change. Iris Young puts this particularly clearly:

On the communicative theory of democracy . . . one function of discussion is precisely to transform people's preferences, to alter or refine their perception of their interests, their perception of the needs and interests of others, their relation to those others, and their perception of collective problems, goals and solutions. Communicative democracy aims to arrive at decisions through persuasion, not merely through the identification and aggregation of existing preferences. By having to speak and justify his or her preferences to others who may be skeptical, a person becomes more reflective about these preferences, accommodates them to the preferences of others, or sometimes becomes even more convinced of the legitimacy of his or her claims.[14]

As the final part of Young's comments reminds us, it would be rather too much to hope that this process of reflective transformation would enable us to resolve all our differences. It will take more than a week of open and public debate for men and women to reach agreement on a fair division of labour between the sexes, or Catholics and Protestants on a fair settlement in Northern Ireland, or Serbs and Croats and Muslims on a new vision of the old Yugoslavia. But when dialogue is opened and differences are more publicly discussed, there is at least some hope of increased mutual understanding—and some chance that a new resolution will emerge.

This is the point of closest contact with the politics of presence, for advocates of deliberative democracy often strengthen their case for a more discussion-based democracy by reference to otherwise

[13]   Mansbridge, 'A Deliberative Theory', 37.
[14]   Young, 'Justice and Communicative Democracy', 129.

intractable problems of difference that get resolved only when we participate in public debate. Deliberation matters only because there *is* difference; if some freak of history or nature had delivered a polity based on unanimous agreement, then politics would be virtually redundant and the decisions would already be made. In the absence of this, deliberative democracy sometimes presents itself as the better way of dealing with group difference. By requiring people to engage more directly with each another, it sets itself against that aggregation of interest that could let the lucky majority get away with whatever it wants. It also enables us to recognize the way that identities are formed through difference, without thereby condemning us to conditions of isolated opposition. 'If', as Amy Gutmann puts it, 'human identity is dialogically created and constituted, then public recognition of our identities requires a politics that leaves room for us to deliberate publicly about those aspects of our identities that we share, or potentially share, with other citizens.' The society that recognizes human identity and difference will then be a 'deliberative democratic society'.[15] All this depends in turn on some guarantee of political presence, for if certain groups have been permanently excluded, the process of deliberation cannot even begin.

I

Both Iris Young and Cass Sunstein have then insisted on the compatibility between deliberative/communicative democracy and guarantees of group representation. Discussion matters, as much as anything, because it offers a way of dislodging existing hierarchies of power. The majoritarian democracy of the ballot box inevitably privileges majorities, and this can have particularly severe consequences for those groups that are in a numerical minority. But this majoritarian democracy also privileges what currently passes for common sense, and this can disempower even those who make up a numerical majority. Women, most notably, have not been able to use the power of their numbers to establish a fairer settlement between the sexes, for their social and economic inequality usually combines with what we might call a cultural inequality which has made it harder for them to challenge the dominant norms. As long as

[15] A. Gutmann, 'Introduction', to A. Gutmann (ed.), *Multiculturalism and the 'Politics of Recognition'*, (Princeton, 1992), 7.

democracies restrict themselves to the 'fair representation' of those preferences that are expressed through the vote, they rule out of court what might emerge under more favourable conditions.

In his discussion of this, Sunstein has particularly emphasized the class dimension: that 'poverty itself is perhaps the most severe obstacle to the free development of preferences and beliefs',[16] and that in the absence of a more deliberative democracy people will not even see what else they could want. Iris Young has been more concerned with the depressing effects of what she calls 'cultural imperialism'[17] on women and those who are in an ethnic or racial minority, and with the way this can force them to formulate their needs in the language of the dominant groups. Both argue that more sustained and open-ended discussion will help raise the profile of groups whose concerns were previously discounted. When a wider set of possibilities is argued and displayed, those who had adjusted their expectations excessively downwards can develop more ambitious hopes or claims. Those who had previously monopolized positions of power and influence might be equally encouraged to recognize their partiality and bias.

Young argues that guaranteed representation for previously marginalized groups is a necessary part of this process: 'where there are social group differences and some groups are privileged and others are oppressed, group representation is necessary to produce a legitimate communicative democratic forum'.[18] Sunstein makes a similar point, arguing that 'deliberative processes will be improved, not undermined, if mechanisms are instituted to ensure that multiple groups have access to the process and are actually present when decisions are made. Proportional or group representation, precisely by having this effect, would ensure that diverse views are expressed on an ongoing basis in the representative process, where they might otherwise be excluded.'[19]

For Sunstein, this is premised on the preference-shaping effects of discussion. If group representation were to be viewed just as a mechanism for the representation of group interest—making sure, as he puts it, that each group gets a 'piece of the action'[20]—then proportional or group representation would look far less attractive. It

---

[16] Sunstein, 'Preferences and Politics', 23.
[17] Young, 'Justice and Communicative Democracy', 133–4.   [18] Ibid. 136.
[19] Sunstein, 'Preferences and Politics', 33.   [20] Ibid.

becomes 'much more acceptable',[21] 'most understandable', in a democracy that refuses to take existing preferences as the last word in what people want; and its real function is 'to ensure that the process of deliberation is not distorted by the mistaken appearance of a common set of interests on the part of all concerned'.[22] Iris Young has been more circumspect on this point, noting that some conflicts of interest between advantaged and disadvantaged groups may be intractable—and, by implication, that it does indeed matter to get a piece of the action. But she too believes that many conflicts are more perceived than real, stemming as much from the ignorance of the privileged groups as from genuine conflicts of interest. 'Privileged groups ignore oppressed groups partly out of prejudice or bigotry, but often simply because they pay sole attention to their own circumstances and apply standards based on their own cultural values'.[23] Where this is so, much can be done simply by changing the people who are present; the subsequent exposure to different experiences or perspectives or values should change the preoccupations of the dominant groups.

There are good grounds for this confidence even in existing political experience, for people do modify and change their opinions when faced with new points of view. The desire to be consistent is a powerful one: once we become convinced, for example, that what others want is similar to what we have claimed for ourselves, we usually feel impelled either to modify our demands or extend our own benefits to others. We may well revise our expectations upwards when we hear what others have regarded as possible; we may also revise our expectations downwards when we recognize conflicting demands or overall constraints. But this latter sometimes seems like a confidence trick, rather than a genuine convergence of opinion and interest. It is the basis, for example, on which some employers have favoured more worker participation in boardroom discussions: that, once the books are opened, the employees will come to recognize that they cannot possibly get what they initially claimed. Where these are the anticipated consequences, we cannot be sure that the outcomes will be just. Those more securely established in existing social hierarchies may still refuse to 'revise their insolent ontologies', and those who survive on the periphery may have their expectations

[21] Ibid.   [22] Ibid. 34.
[23] Young, 'Justice and Communicative Democracy', 136.

raised only to find them more severely dashed. And in some contexts there really is a zero-sum game: I cannot see how women can achieve equal pay with men without men losing their pay differentials; nor can I see how black Americans can achieve equal employment opportunities with white without white Americans losing some existing advantage. Young notes that 'where the total wage pool grows, male or white workers need not lose anything through pay equity adjustments'.[24] But at a time when many economies face high and continuing levels of unemployment, as well as increased patterns of segmentation within their labour force, this is not entirely convincing.

Part of the project of deliberative democracy has been to dislodge individual and group interest from their dominant positions on the political stage, and while both Sunstein and Young see this as compatible with principles of group representation, the proposed compatibility depends on what might seem an overly optimistic scenario of mutual adjustment and change. For those who do not even address the mechanics of representation, the detachment from reality has been still more marked. Explorations of deliberative or communicative democracy often refer rather grandly to a principle of equal access to decision-making assemblies or substantive equality in resources and power, but they do not give much consistent attention to how these conditions would ever be achieved. Jurgen Habermas, for one, insists that all those affected by a decision must be enabled to participate 'as free and equal members in a co-operative search for truth in which only the force of the better argument may hold sway',[25] and that the only test of a valid judgement is whether its consequences and side-effects meet the free consent of all those affected. This seems to attach decisive importance to the principle of equal access, but Habermas remains relatively incurious about what might be necessary to deliver on this. Indeed, his work is littered with the kind of 'let us assume' constructions that are more typically associated with economic than political theory.[26] And this is not, I

[24] Young, 'Justice and Communicative Democracy', 136.

[25] J. Habermas, cited in G. Warnke, *Justice and Interpretation* (Cambridge, 1992), 91.

[26] E.g. in a recent essay on 'Struggles for Recognition in Constitutional States', *European Journal of Philosophy*, 1/2 (1993), 141: 'Let us assume that a well-functioning public sphere with structures of communication that are not distorted by power and which permit and promote discourses of self-understanding can thus

think, just an oversight; for, when the mechanisms on offer edge too closely towards defining participants as representatives of distinct and separate group interests, this can threaten the conditions for free communication. If group representatives really are there to represent their group, this must put limits on subsequent modifications of their initial position.

II

If the point of group representation is to represent previously ignored or disadvantaged interests, the representatives cannot just take it into their heads to abandon the commitments they brought with them when they joined the representative assembly. They can make some minor adjustments in the light of the subsequent discussion, and most of those they claim to represent will accept the legitimacy of this. Anything more substantial, however, would have to be referred back to the original group. The group, of course, will not have had the benefit of exposure to deliberative diversity and discussion, and might be considerably less willing to bow to the 'power of the better argument'. But even if the representatives manage to convince them, this is hardly the process deliberative democrats have in mind. Deliberative assemblies are not normally conceived on the model of industrial relations, where the negotiators break off discussion in order to consult with their members; on the contrary, the participants must have considerable autonomy to change their point of view. As Joshua Cohen puts it:

Ideal deliberation is *free* in that it satisfies two conditions. First, the participants regard themselves as bound only by the results of their deliberation and by the precondition for that deliberation. Their consideration of proposals is not constrained by the authority of prior norms or requirements. Second, the participants suppose that they can act from the results, taking the fact that a certain decision is arrived at through their deliberation as a sufficient reason for complying with it.[27]

If this is what deliberation implies, it is surely at odds with any notions of group representation, for the process cannot have its

develop in such multicultural societies against the background of a liberal culture and on the basis of voluntary associations.'

[27] Cohen, 'Deliberation and Democratic Legitimacy', 22.

desired effects if people are bound by previous mandates. Representatives cannot arrive on the scene with their hands tied to the pursuit of pre-agreed, fixed, group interests: if this were the case, they would be refusing the power of subsequent discussion. Participants in a deliberative democracy have to be freed from stricter forms of political accountability if they are to be freed to engage in discussion.

This retreat from strict notions of representation and accountability is at first sight rather startling, and the accusation may seem particularly unfair as applied to Iris Young's work, which has been consistently characterized by a concern with the self-organization of representative groups. But the different balance that is then struck between accountability and autonomy is, I believe, crucial to any politics of presence, and it helps secure its association with the project of deliberative democracy. No plausible theory of representation can afford to discount questions of accountability: representatives who are in no way accountable are not representative at all. But the accountability that is secured in advance is by definition confined to the politics of ideas, for it is only by reference to explicitly set out programmes and policies that we can think of our representatives as bound to certain courses of action. The accountability that is achieved after the event is a bit more complicated. We may hold our representatives to account for all kinds of things they did in our name, including many they never said they would do, and then make a retrospective judgement about how well they managed to represent us. This retrospective holding to account also takes place, however, within the framework of a politics of ideas, for our judgements will be based on specific policies and actions. What the politics of presence insists on is an additional element of 'representativeness' which gets squeezed out in the exclusive focus on the content of policies and programmes. This addititional element is not amenable to the same mechanisms of accountability.

Against this background, the deliberative retreat from stricter notions of accountability should not be viewed as a failure of democratic integrity. On the contrary, it gives extra theoretical legitimacy to the implications of a politics of presence, and it is at this point that it most usefully meets up with the arguments of this book.

Accountability has been a crucial and positive value in what I have argued so far, and has figured large in my assessment of what it means for women to be 'represented' by women, or black people by 'representatives' who are black. If the presumption is that all women or all black people share the same preferences and goals, this is clearly—and dangerously—erroneous. It has the effect of absolving the so-called representatives from any responsibility for finding out what those they represent actually want, and it lends a spurious air of legitimacy to people whose preferred policies may be completely unrepresentative. Notions of authentic or organic representation should simply be ruled out of court: these can never be the basis for an alternative system of representation.

But the representation of people just in accordance with their expressed ideas is also unsatisfactory, and especially when the only vehicles for this representation are the catch-all parties currently on offer. The programmes offered by competing political parties can never capture the full range of relevant issues, and once we abandon the illusion that representatives who agree with us on one point will also share our views on another, it becomes necessary to pursue some additional form of representation that deals with as yet unspecified areas of concern. I have argued that the gender and racial composition of elected assemblies is one important additional 'guarantee', but what this guarantees remains ambiguous when it is not tied to specific ideas. This is particularly apparent in the case of gender quotas, where there is a clear expectation that women representatives will do more, or other, than was promised in their party's election campaign. It is less obvious in the politics around minority representation in the USA, where there is a stronger connection with specific voting districts, and where national party disciplines tend to be weaker; this makes it possible for candidates to contest elections on programmes explicitly tied to minority concerns. But in either case, the preference for representatives who represent not only through a congruity in political ideas but also through an additional element of shared experience seems to edge back to uncomfortable notions of authentic or organic representation. What else is it that makes them accountable, other than false claims about shared identity?

In the analysis of gender quotas, I argued that part of what has to change in the framing of such questions is the obsession with political guarantees. Failing an explicitly woman-friendly programme (which men might then legitimately claim they were equally capable of pursuing), there *is* no guarantee that women will represent women's interests. The only other guarantee would be an essential unity of women, and this is not a presumption I favour. Failing either of these, gender parity is, in one sense, a shot in the dark. The value attached to an increased presence of women within decision-making assemblies derives from a more general (and inevitably more tenuous) perception of those values and goals and perspectives that most women develop out of the experiences that differentiate them from most men. This is not strictly representation, nor is it strictly accountable. On the other hand, it does mesh quite neatly with what is being claimed for deliberative democracy.

When I argue that the sex or race or ethnicity of the representatives matters—over and above whatever they have promised to do—I necessarily take issue with the politics of binding mandates or any exclusive emphasis on tying the representatives' hands. This can go only so far, which is largely an empirical judgement. And it should go only so far, for, while all democracies have to keep representatives accountable to their officially declared policies, this is not the only thing democracies need. We also need to be represented in ways that will get new issues on to the political agenda, and will challenge the false consensus that keeps so many out. If all the options were already in play, or all needs and preferences already clearly defined, then the priority would more properly lie with getting more vigorous advocates. This certainly plays its part in the argument for more women in politics, and it plays an even greater part in the argument for minority representation in the USA; but all those pressing the inclusion of the previously excluded also stress the hegemonic power of dominant perspectives and the way these have blocked thinking on what else could be done. In her discussion of the 'five faces of oppression', Iris Young lists exploitation, marginalization, powerlessness, cultural imperialism, and violence, any one of which, she argues, marks out a group as oppressed, but all of which can exist together.[28] This potentially multi-layered experience does not translate in any automatic way into neatly laid out programmes of action: like all translations, there are first attempts and repeated revisions, and no guarantees of a satisfactory final result. Where so much new thinking has to be done, there is not a great deal to be guaranteed,

---

[28] Young, *Justice and the Politics of Difference*, ch. 2.

and while the representatives we entrust with this work have to be subject to all the usual mechanisms of dismissal and recall, we cannot expect to know all they will do in advance.

Let me put the same point from the opposite direction. When needs or interests have crystallized in the form of explicit policy proposals, we are back in the more familiar territory of political ideas, and can draw on the more familiar conventions of political accountability to ensure that our representatives really do represent us. On this terrain, it may be relatively unimportant whether those pressing for the policies are male or female, white or black, Latino or Jewish or Catholic; what matters is that the people elected on this platform then do what they said they would do. The representation of minority interests in the USA, for example, could then be genuinely detached from the increased representation of minority politicians, for what would matter would be the strength of commitment to a particular package of reforms, regardless of one's ethnic identity. Now, if the overall composition of the legislatures remained predominantly white, minority Americans might still query this strength of commitment; they might legitimately feel, both for symbolic reasons and as an extra guarantee of vigorous advocacy, that they still needed more minority politicians. More importantly, they might also argue that it was necessary to increase the number of minority politicians as a way of protecting themselves against future developments which could require some quick thinking about minority interests. The autonomy we must allow our politicians—and even more so, from a deliberative perspective—only becomes legitimate when we have some additional basis for believing them representative. The greater the autonomy, the greater the importance we have to attach to equal or proportionate presence. If the representatives were only messengers, sent there to pass on pre-agreed programmes and ideas, then it might seem rather beside the point to worry about how many of them are female or Latino or black. But if the representatives are to claim considerable autonomy, we will more legitimately worry about how much of our experience they share.

What deliberative democracy brings to the fore is that representatives need some such autonomy. Preferences, interests, and goals are shaped by the conditions out of which they arise, and if we condemn our politicians to tedious reiteration of what we told them to say, we refuse the possibility of any later transformation. The politics of binding mandates, for example, relies on a static universe in which preferences have to be taken as given, and when representatives stray too far from their original positions, this is commonly regarded as a form of betrayal. Though this is one way of thinking about representation, it is neither the only nor most useful one. Representation has to include both accountability and relative autonomy, otherwise we are reduced to mere aggregation of initial preference and interest.

III

That said, there remains some considerable ambiguity over how far deliberative democracy can accommodate the determined pursuit of group interest. This is a separate question from the role of binding mandates or the degree of autonomy we allow our representatives: it is more a matter of how they should conceive of their role. The critique of strict accountability can come from a number of directions. In his argument for democracy by sampling, for example, John Burnheim also challenges the preoccupation with controlling representatives by binding them to professed opinions or ideas: indeed, he is far more explicit on this point than most advocates of deliberative democracy.[29] But he bases his argument on what is almost the opposite principle: that 'nobody should have any input into decision-making where they have no legitimate material interest'.[30] Representation is then equated with the representation of interest, which Burnheim presents as safer and more democratic than accountability through political views; as he rather plausibly puts it, 'I should prefer my interests to be safeguarded rather than have my more or less shaky opinions prevail.'[31] His 'demarchy' involves a statistical representation of the relevant parties to any decision, which he defines in functional terms as those who work at producing a good, those who consume it, and those who are affected by its side-effects. Accountability is not the issue for Burnheim: '[d]emarchic leaders would not be accountable because they would not be eligible for reappointment'.[32] We would, however, have good grounds for trusting them, because they share our interests.

Though Burnheim does not address the more tangled questions arising from representations of race or gender, his preoccupations

---

[29] Burnheim, *Is Democracy Possible?* (Cambridge, 1985).
[30] Ibid. 5.   [31] Ibid. 112.   [32] Ibid. 167.

clearly overlap with those of the politics of presence. But where Sunstein or Young put their case for proportional or group representation in the context of a deliberative democracy, Burnheim makes interest the cornerstone of his. Other than this, the positions are not poles apart: Burnheim queries the status of those preferences that are expressed through the ballot box, noting that people often lack the information that would enable them to decide what they want; he anticipates a far more participatory and discussion-based democracy than the one achieved through existing representative democracy; and he expects representatives of the different interests to develop and refine their positions. But their legitimacy is grounded in their interests. They are there to speak to the needs and concerns of their group.

In the characterizations of the ideal deliberative procedure, by contrast, 'the members of the association are committed to resolving their differences through deliberation, and thus to provide reasons that they sincerely expect to be persuasive to others who share that commitment'.[33] This is said to rule out any simple insistence on what groups need or want, for how could anyone seriously expect mere assertions of need to be sufficiently persuasive to the others? It is also said to rule out 'efforts to disguise personal or class advantage as the common advantage',[34] for such deceptions simply fail to meet the proposed commitment to deliberated resolutions. As Joshua Cohen goes on to argue, this is not really something that can be settled by stipulation, and the more substantive claim is that people *will* modify their preferences when they find they cannot defend them in reasonable discussion. It is at this point that we may find ourselves worrying about what happens to specific group interests. It is also at this point that Iris Young's reservations about the language of deliberation become particularly compelling,[35] for there might be all kinds of reasons why we fail to make our arguments persuasive, and these may have little to do with the legitimacy of our initial claims.

One widely remarked phenomenon of representative democracy is the incorporation of the radical outsider: people get themselves elected on programmes of far-reaching reform, but then conform to the very practices they had so vigorously attacked. One way of thinking of this is that they have excelled in the arts of deliberation,

[33] Cohen, 'Deliberation and Democratic Legitimacy', 24.
[34] Ibid.   [35] Young, 'Justice and Communicative Democracy'.

but thereby lost sight of their original ground. The good deliberator is not necessarily the best of advocates, for the more we try to enter into other people's positions or adapt our arguments to what they will find persuasive, the more we may detach ourselves from the community whose interests we initially shared. We become drawn into a reasonable consensus, and no longer fight our own local patch. Valuable as this often is, it can also work to reinforce the previous exclusions. Those on the outside had their moment of entry; now they are back where they were, with no one who will speak to their cause.

There is an important sense in which democracies need advocates as well as deliberators: they may need both the intransigent narrowness of those who will not budge from their initial positions and the more comprehensive vision of those who adjust what they want to what they come to see as reasonable and possible. A politics based exclusively on the first would be a disaster. But a politics based exclusively on the second tends to converge around a less imaginative consensus, and this often reproduces the limitations of the past. We are unlikely to find the two characteristics combined in a single representative,[36] though we may find many who pass through both stages in the course of their political lives. This is part of the impetus behind proposals for rotation in office (one element in Burnheim's scheme), for, as each fiery advocate is transformed into yet another reasonable deliberator, we look for that extra energy and determination that comes with the more recently elected. As long as society is composed of groups with different and conflicting interests, we will continue to need those representatives who constitute themselves as representing the needs and interests of such groups. And, while many of the anticipated conflicts may reveal themselves as more apparent than real, some may be genuinely intractable—episodes in a zero-sum game.

The worst scenario, perhaps, is when conflicts are indeed intractable, but the participants in discussion still reach agreement on what is really a false consensus. Theorists of deliberative democracy have not given adequate attention to the power play at work inside what passes for rational discussion; the way that a 'certain *culture* of deliberation' can privilege some resolutions and make others

[36] This is one of the key messages I take from Joseph Raz's work on the plurality of virtues: J. Raz, *The Morality of Freedom* (Oxford, 1986).

seem beyond the pale. 'It is no secret', as Iris Young remarks, 'that in actual communication situations in our society, poor, or less educated, or non-professionals, or privatized people are often intimidated by the discourse rules of formal organizations, and their speech is often not taken seriously and deemed rational by those organizations.'[37] The priority attached to reasonable resolution can then undermine the equality of access, and the power that ought to come with presence can be seriously reduced.

IV

The association between deliberative democracy and the project of changing the gender and ethnic composition of elected assemblies thus remains uneasy, if close. The closeness is more surprising than the distance, given that deliberative models have arisen out of an explicit critique of the politics based around interest, while the politics of presence has stressed the representation of interest as one part, if not all, of its goal. And the connection is more than formal; it is not just that both stress equality of access, or that both address the problem of political exclusion. In their critical evaluation of the preferences that are expressed through the vote, theorists of deliberative democracy confirm the reservations about contemporary practices of representation, and open up the necessary space for considering 'who' represents us as well as 'what' preferences or ideas they carry. In their analysis of what it means to participate in deliberative procedures, they also provide a clearer theoretical basis for what is otherwise rather a conundrum about political accountability. Accountability to pre-agreed policies or commitments can only ever be part of what democracy is about, and in the more open-ended deliberations through which the final decisions are made, the representatives have to lay claim to some considerable autonomy. If this autonomy is not to become a recipe for their total independence, however, we need the additional confidence that derives from changing the composition of the decision-making assemblies. Achieving gender parity, or a more proportionate distribution of political office between the different ethnic groups within the society, is no *guarantee* of this—democratic politics rarely offers guarantees. But

---

[37] Young, 'Justice and Communicative Democracy', 127.

autonomy seems totally illegitimate when the representatives are drawn from a narrowly defined group or caste.

This point remains largely implicit in most of the arguments for deliberative democracy, where the recurrent anxieties about giving too much weight to specifically group interest often blocks more detailed recommendations for the composition of the deliberating assembly. Rian Voet, for example, steers clears of what she sees as the cruder policy of gender quotas for legislative assemblies, fearing that this would cement an essentialist politics of group representation, and prevent people addressing the common good.[38] While she is seriously exercised over women's under-participation in politics, she then prefers to limit quotas to internal party arrangements, relying elsewhere on a (vaguer) republican formulation that each must be ruler and ruled in turn. Others who work within a deliberative or civic republican framework tend to fall back on some general rubric about equal access or equality of resources, and elements of group representation are seriously incorporated only in the versions developed by Cass Sunstein and Iris Marion Young.

The outcomes of deliberation are more often said to derive their legitimacy from having followed the appropriate procedures; thus, people have to give reasons for whatever they propose, and they have to accept the results of the more powerful argument. Though this is clearly intended to reduce the power of vested interests, the emphasis on procedural legitimacy can lead to an under-emphasis on the actual composition of the decision-making assembly: equality remains on the list, but may not be very prominently displayed. The attachment to reasonable discussion can also underplay the continuing importance of advocacy, and this can make it more difficult for groups to assert a distinct group interest. As Jane Mansbridge has argued in many different explorations of the relationship between consensual and protective democracy, the conditions that most enhance deliberation and consensus are not always so good at achieving a fair distribution between groups that are actually in conflict, and we may need 'institutions based primarily on self-

---

[38] M. C. B. Voet, 'Political Representation and Quotas: Hanna Pitkin's Concept(s) of Representation in the Context of Feminist Politics', *Acta Politica*, 27/4 (1992); also M. C. B. Voet, 'Women as Citizens: A Feminist Debate', *Australian Feminist Studies*, 19 (1994).

interest as well as those based primarily on altruism'.[39] Where the attachment to deliberative procedures threatens to weaken one element in this necessary balance, it can undermine the claims of the most oppressed groups. We cannot rule interest out of politics, nor should we yet see this as a desirable aim.

[39] J. J. Mansbridge, 'The Rise and Fall of Self-Interest in the Explanation of Political Life', in J. J. Mansbridge (ed.), *Beyond Self-Interest* (Chicago, 1990), 21; see also her concluding argument in J. J. Mansbridge, *Beyond Adversary Democracy* (New York, 1980).

CHAPTER 7

Loose ends and larger ambitions

In my opening chapter, I identified three major objections that are levelled at a politics of presence. The first was that giving additional weight to characteristics such as gender or ethnicity could over-politicize group difference, thereby disrupting social cohesion or political stability. The second was that making representation even partially dependent on such characteristics could weaken the basis for political accountability. The third was that reinforcing the role of group interest in politics could undermine a more generous politics aimed at a general interest or shared concerns. The resolution to all of these lies in the precise status to be attached to notions of 'group representation'. I have argued for active intervention to include members of groups currently under-represented in politics, but I have sought to drive a wedge between this and stricter notions of group representation. My arguments certainly anticipate that changing the composition of decision-making bodies changes the character of the issues and policies discussed. They do not, however, presume that such representatives pursue a homogeneous or static group interest. The politics of presence is not about locking people into pre-given, essentialized identities; nor is it just a new way of defining the interest groups that should jostle for attention. The point, rather, is to enable those now excluded from politics to engage more directly in political debate and political decision.

Although these arguments apply with equal force to each of the case studies pursued in this book, the politics of presence points towards rather different policy recommendations depending on the nature of the excluded group. In relation to women, a straightforward quota seems entirely appropriate. Although gender quotas remain highly controversial, this is, on the whole, because they introduce significant elements of positive action; they are not additionally regarded as a serious threat to social cohesion or political stability. Gender quotas do not presume any unified 'women's position'; indeed, the shift from a more token representation of women opens up space for a wide variety of female politicians, only some of whom will feel themselves charged with responsibility for speaking for women as a whole. The problems associated with gender quotas are, in my view, largely pragmatic. Thus, in electoral systems that operate through single-member constituencies, and in party systems that allow the local constituency the main voice in candidate selection (both of these being features of the British system), it is impossible to impose a national quota without overriding local choice. In such contexts, quotas have to operate as a stronger version of targets—which is effectively what is happening in the British Labour Party today.

In comparison with racial or ethnic quotas, the introduction of minimum quotas for women and men is also less inherently problematic because there are self-evidently two sexes. Sexual difference keeps changing its historical meaning—this is no mere 'fact' of human biology—but it still revolves around a relatively uncontroversial distinction between women and men. Ethnic difference, by contrast, is far more intrinsically contested. Most discussions distinguish between an ethnic majority and ethnic minori*ties*, and these ethnic minorities then lend themselves to a process of ever more precise subdivision. 'New ethnicities' are also continually being created—through intermarriage, through cultural transmission, through the myriad complexities of individual choice. It is only in the most unusual of conditions that a society divides into two distinct ethnic groups (I cannot think of a single instance in the world today), and, outside of these conditions, ethnic quotas will always fail to capture the diversity of ethnic identities. When these elements are combined with the disturbing historical associations that attach to racial or ethnic quotas, it is difficult to justify quotas as the best way of dealing with racial or ethnic exclusions.

The alternative strategy adopted in the USA has stressed the right to elect 'representatives of one's choice', and has relied on redistricting arrangements to deliver some approximation to proportionate presence. As already noted, this strategy may have reached its historical limits; for, while the geographical concentration of minority voters has allowed for a significant number of 'majority–minority' districts, the total cannot be substantially raised without recourse to 'bizarrely' shaped electoral districts. This raises the prospect of a more explicit quota policy, but none of the authors discussed in Chapter 4 has argued in favour of this. In the American context at least, racial quotas are considered neither possible nor desirable.

The only partial exception that surfaces in this book relates to the under-representation of Aboriginal peoples in Canadian politics, and the widely canvassed proposals for guaranteed seats in a reformed Senate. The rights of indigenous peoples are often thought to raise issues that do not translate readily to other minority groups, partly because of the history of dispossession, and partly because indigenous peoples are seen as more self-evidently distinct in their cultural and political traditions. Even here, it may be said, questions arise about the definition of 'Aboriginal peoples', and how any system of guaranteed representation can balance the claims of the different groups contained within this description. When applied to the representation of other kinds of ethnic minority, setting a minimum quota for political office seems to raise more questions than it resolves.

In much of contemporary Europe, the category of 'ethnic minority' covers a wide spectrum of differently constituted groups; and, while members of each minority may feel themselves inadequately represented by members of the ethnic majority, they may feel themselves equally ill-represented by members of another ethnic minority. Attaching specific numbers to specified minority groups then becomes an unenviable task. Between the risks, on the one hand, of a simplistic dualism that distinguishes only between the ethnic majority and the rest, and the absurdities, on the other hand, of an endless quest for sufficiently pluralized categories, it is hardly surprising that quotas have won so little popular support.

Achieving proportionate presence for ethnic minorities is then a more complex process than achieving parity between two sexes. In each case, the first stage is to win support for the principles of a politics of presence: to achieve wider public and party recognition than the representative's race, ethnicity, or sex are matters of political concern. But whereas this recognition can translate into relatively straightforward numerical quotas by sex, it requires greater flexibility in the case of ethnicity or race. This suggests, perhaps, a policy of targets rather than quotas: something that recognizes the difficulty of attaching definitive numbers to a constantly shifting pattern of different ethnic groups, and is more attuned to the changing nature of ethnic identities. It also strengthens more general arguments in favour of multi-member electoral districts, and voting systems based on proportional representation. Any such developments fall considerably short of the kind of guarantee that can be delivered by gender quotas. The danger, of course, is that this can undermine the urgency attached to changing the ethnic composition of elected assemblies, and can push this project into the realm of the distantly desirable rather than the immediately required. I have, as yet, no answer to this.

The issues raised by territorial or linguistic minorities further complicate the policy implications. As the Canadian example indicates, political presence cannot be regarded as the exclusive route to meeting what may be very different perceptions of political marginality, and it seems particularly inappropriate when what is at issue is incorporation into a majority norm. The Canadian example also reinforces an argument that has been made throughout the book: that recommendations on institutional design have to be tailored to local conditions, with a keen eye to the historical background and the likely consequences of future change. The theoretical arguments merely establish the validity of presence as part of the process of representation. It would be foolhardy to deduce a single set of policies that can be applied to each situation.

I

Though I cannot claim that my arguments have resolved all remaining queries around these points, I want to turn now to what I see as the most obvious loose ends. The first of these relates to the as yet unsettled role of class; the second, to those alternative strategies for democratization that can be roughly categorized as projects for spreading democracy more fully around; the third, to the under-representation of disadvantaged or minority groups in other institutions of government. I have focused primarily on the under-representation of women and people from ethnic or racial minorities, and I have considered their under-representation in relation to existing layers of elected government. This narrows—perhaps unnecessarily—the scope and implications of my argument. How far is it open to further extension?

On the first point, it might be said that I have engaged in some rather fancy footwork around who qualifies for political presence. I have distinguished my argument from those more general notions of mirror or descriptive representation, which might require the reflection of each and every characteristic of the citizenry inside the governing assemblies; and I have argued that all serious claims to guaranteed representation have to be grounded in something more than a statistical mismatch between voters and those who represent them. There has to be an additional analysis of existing structures of exclusion, which then serves to identify the areas of most pressing concern. This might be grounded in the inequities of the sexual division of labour, which lend a false air of normality to the under-representation of women among those seeking political office; or it might be grounded in the historical formation of particular nations, which built themselves on denying racial equality, or the displacement of entire peoples.

This works well enough against facetious claims for the proportionate representation of people with blue eyes and red hair. It should also, though more contentiously, work to discredit the claims of previously dominant groups who see their relative advantage slipping from their grasp. But the most persistent structure of political exclusion is surely that associated with inequalities of social class, and this is the one form of social division and inequality that has been remarkably absent from my discussion. How do I justify this silence on divisions and exclusions by class? Is this just another example of that contemporary displacement which has pushed class so far out of the picture? Or are there significant differences between class on the one hand and gender, ethnicity, or race on the other, which help make sense of this move?

One easy, but also disingenuous, answer is that representatives do not change their gender or ethnic identity when they are elected to political office, but do modify their class position. The unemployed can hardly demand representation by people without jobs, nor those living in poverty by people who are equally poor; for, once political representation becomes a full-time activity, it carries with it a salary, and the scale of remuneration is always set at a level considerably above the average wage. The use of public funds to pay elected representatives was indeed an early radical demand, designed to dislodge those with private sources of income from their previous monopoly, and to open up political office to people with no money of their own. Socialists used to argue that this payment should correspond to average wages (this was one of the principles that Marx and Lenin, for example, derived from the Paris Commune), but this is not practised anywhere in the democratic world. In terms of both income and employment, those elected to decision-making assemblies enjoy a relatively privileged position, and this makes it harder for them to claim themselves as true representatives of the working class.

Defining class by income is a rather suspect simplification, however, and representatives who originate from the working class will not necessarily change their cultural or political identities just because they now earn more money than their peers. The unemployed or the poor could certainly ask to be represented by people with a prior experience of poverty or unemployment, and those in manual employment could equally well lay claim to representation by people with a prior experience of manual labour. The British Labour MP, Aneurin Bevan, used to say that full representation was achieved only when the people elected 'spoke with the authentic accents' of those who elected them, and were 'in touch with their realities';[1] this appeal to shared experience seems as legitimate in the case of class as it does in the case of gender or race. Neither the past nor present condition of such representatives is likely to be wholly 'representative'; in the British experience, those MPs or councillors who can best claim to be working-class often have an untypical trajectory which may take in years as a trade union organizer or significant periods in higher education. But if the general case for political presence stands, it is not clear why it should be limited to women or those who are in a racial or ethnic minority. One of the recurrent complaints against guaranteed representation for members of particular social groups is that this can become a vehicle for more self-interested career advancement. Extending the argument to take

[1] Quoted in A. Arblaster, *Democracy* (Milton Keynes, 1987), 84. Bevan was a member of the post-war Labour government, and saw himself as an authentic spokesman for the working class.

in guaranteed representation by class would go some way towards settling this suspicion, and would make it more abundantly clear that the politics of presence involves a critique of political élites.

A more subtle, but perhaps equally disingenuous, argument is that 'working class' is an empty category, a term that suggests more substantial unity of interests and priorities than is ever justified by political events, 'a signifier without a signified'.[2] Since much of my argument has been concerned with challenging equally suspect assumptions of unity around categories such as female or black, this is hardly a definitive objection. My own understanding of demands for equal or proportionate presence detaches them from any presumed grounding in essential identities, and argues that any politics of presence should work in tandem with the equally pressing politics of competing ideas. Group interests, needs, preferences, or perspectives do not come to us ready-made by material conditions, and their representation is never absolved from processes of internal contestation and debate. If this is true, as it undoubtedly is, for those disparate groupings we may gather together under the heading of 'working class', it is equally, if not more, true for women, for black or Latino Americans, for Aboriginal women and men, for francophone or anglophone Canadians. This undermines suspect notions of 'authentic' or 'organic' representation, but it does not dent the general case for equal or proportionate presence.

If there *is* a basis for distinction, it lies in the historically greater importance attached to class issues and class concerns. Working-class people have always been marginal to the circulation of political élites, but, as a principle for defining the major options in political life, class itself has had an extraordinary presence. For much of the last two centuries, class has operated as the organizing symbol for defining the political spectrum, dividing parties and movements according to their stance on competition and co-operation, capitalism and socialism, the free market and planning, private property and social equality. As historians of the nineteenth and twentieth century have shown,[3] this could hardly have happened without a

---

[2] E. Laclau, 'Why Do Empty Signifiers Matter to Politics?', in J. Weeks (ed.), *The Lesser Evil and the Greater Good* (London, 1994), 167. As the title of Laclau's essay indicates, he is not saying that empty signifiers have no substance to the way that politics may develop.

[3] Most notably E. P. Thompson, in *The Making of the English Working Class* (London, 1963).

powerful organizing impetus from working-class constituencies and groups: class did not erupt on the scene just as a tool for social or economic analysis. But the alternatives that were derived from experiences of dispossession, poverty, unemployment, or deepening inequality did then develop a life of their own. Class came to exist on at least three, potentially separate, levels: it became a form of social analysis; a way of describing the conditions to which working-class people were subjected; and a promise of a new kind of political identity. Marxists have frequently talked of the difference between a 'class in itself' and a 'class for itself', the first referring to an objective unity that stems from shared relations of production, and the second to the moment when that unity becomes the self-conscious basis for political solidarity and action. But class has also been the nexus around which people organize their competing analyses of social conditions and competing programmes for social and economic change. It became the code-word for a new set of political ideas.

In the conventional triad of race, class, and gender, class then stands out as the one most detachable from experiences of oppression or exploitation. To say this is not just to restate the widely remarked phenomena of the bourgeois socialist and the working-class conservative. The class origins of those who identify with socialist or social democratic politics have always been astonishingly diverse (as, indeed, have been the class origins of those who identify with its opposite); but shared experience is never a guarantee of shared political beliefs, and class is only one of many demonstrations of this. The roll-call of the men who have thrown themselves into struggles for sexual equality may be rather short, but many white people campaigned for the abolition of black slavery in the Americas, or joined in the later campaigns for black civil rights. People's political priorities and beliefs do not simply reflect personal needs or material conditions. The point about class is that it entered so thoroughly into the definition of political policies and programmes (most notably, though not exclusively, in Europe) that it did become more readily detachable from claims to political presence.

In terms of electoral politics in particular, what started as a movement for the representation of labour (labouring men *and* labour interest) has fallen victim to its own success. Though many regret the declining proportion of trade unionists or manual workers among those elected to local or national office, there is relatively little support for the notion that only workers can be trusted to devise appropriate policies for social equality, or that only those with a prior experience of poverty or homelessness or unemployment can know what is best to be done. The uncertainty that many have expressed in relation to policies on gender or race or the treatment of indigenous peoples—that sense of not really knowing without asking what it is that these people might want—has no strong parallel here; and the under-representation of the poor or those in manual employment is more commonly conceived in terms of the lack of vigour with which their interests are pursued. It is not that existing representatives are thought incapable of indentifying either the problems or the solutions, but that they may not be sufficiently affected by the experiences to be trusted to carry the policies through.

The under-representation by social class is most commonly perceived in these terms, and does not then share that additional quality which lies behind current pressures for political presence. Those who argue for the proportional representation of women, or of men and women from ethnic or racial minorities, are concerned primarily with the construction of a new political agenda, with the articulation of previously unheard voices, and the development of new priorities and tasks. The demands would lose some of their urgency if the political agenda already incorporated the interests and perspectives of these groups, and would have to fall back on the symbolic significance of achieving equal or proportionate representation, combined with the requirement for more vigorous advocacy. Though I have noted throughout that these are important elements in the arguments for political presence, I have continued to attach most weight to the policy changes that are anticipated from modifying the composition of political élites. This, in turn, reflects the relationship I favour between ideas and political presence. If all that matters is being there, with no further implication about the new policies we might expect to emerge, then 'who' the representatives are becomes entirely distinct from 'what' we want those representatives to do, and the proposed reforms become a vehicle for cultural rather than political intervention. If, on the contrary, the social or sexual characteristics of the representatives are regarded as a sufficient guarantee that they will perform as advocates for those who share these characteristics, ideas still drop out of the picture, and we are left with essentialist predictions about what generates political action. The real importance of political presence lies in the way it is thought to transform the political agenda, and it is this that underlies the greater priority now accorded to gender and ethnicity and race.

The frequent use of the term 'perspectives' is revealing here, for it reinforces that sense of issues not yet precisely delineated and priorities still to be defined. Class, by contrast, has been more typically discussed in terms of objective interest. Marxism, for example, developed an analysis of the objective conflicts of interest that were grounded in relations of production, and, despite troubled explorations of the conditions under which a 'class in itself' would turn into a 'class for itself', continued to regard these interests as independent of anyone's perception. One implication was that you did not need to experience exploitation in order to know what it meant; indeed, in Lenin's analysis of the role of intellectuals in revolutionary politics, experience of only one aspect of oppression or exploitation would engender a blinkered reformism that could not make the necessary connections. This more theoretically driven understanding of interests allows for representation (or leadership) by people other than those most directly concerned, but, in the subsequent shift to non-class bases of difference, the language of interests was supplanted by a rather different language of perspectives or approaches or concerns. The 'interests' of workers or pensioners or the long-term unemployed can perhaps be championed by those who fall into none of these categories. It is hard to see how the 'perspectives' of women or black Americans can be articulated, except through representatives who are female or black; and this requirement is even more pressing when we consider what may be fundamental differences of value, as in the relationship of indigenous peoples to the natural world. The case for presence is particularly powerful when it addresses those ideas or concerns or values that have not yet reached the political stage, or when it looks at preferences not yet formulated and possibilities not yet explored. Because of its prior dominance, class does not fall so neatly into any of these categories.

Though I say this with some trepidation, I believe that the above does provide a basis for distinguishing between the political exclusions associated with class and the political exclusions associated with gender or race. It also, however, indicates important areas of overlap. Objective analysis of class interest or class conflict tends to operate at a level of generality which leaves many considerations untouched, and there is still a sense in which the under-representation of working-class 'perspectives' can lead to policies that override or ignore working-class concerns. In the post-war reconstruction of Britain, for example, inner-city (often bomb-damaged) slums were torn down, and new housing estates were rapidly erected to provide workers with improved accommodation. But the forcible relocation of entire communities to what later became the 'sink' estates of the 1960s and 1970s was neither an architectural nor a social success, and many have attributed the failures of post-war planning to the lack of consultation with the people whose lives were being arbitrarily transformed. Those who developed the policies may have been thoroughly committed to what they saw as working-class interest, but in their top-down analysis of objective need, they failed to engage with what local people could have articulated as their immediate concerns.

The critique of post-war planning has obvious parallels with feminist critiques which stress the under-representation of women in the formulation of public policy. In both cases, what is at issue *is* the construction of the political agenda, and the way that the composition of the policy-makers can limit the range of perspectives and concerns. Where policy alternatives can be established with all the rigidity of 'objective' conditions, then political presence may be more of an optional extra, or something with primarily symbolic effects. There is no real substitute for being there when new policies are being developed—and no real basis, at this point, for differentiating between gender and class.

Examples drawn from housing, however, or the broader area of urban or regional renewal, tend to focus attention on the under-representation of local or community voices: the emphasis is on failures in *local* consultation or representation, rather than on an under-representation at national level. When contemporary theorists address the problem of class-based exclusion, this is usually the level at which they work, linking the more direct representation of working-class people and concerns to some form of decentralization. This could be viewed just as capitulation to political reality; for, however controversial the guaranteed representation of women or ethnic minorities is proving, it is in many ways less threatening to current practices of democracy than guaranteed representation by social class. Most of those who benefit from gender quotas, for example, will resemble the current incumbents of political office in their occupational or class characteristics, and this makes it easier to include them as new members of the political family. This bow to political reality is partially shored up by the fact that class already defines the political agenda. But the exclusion of working-class *perspectives* seems just as problematic for contemporary democracy as the exclusion of women or ethnic minorities—and, indeed, goes a long way towards explaining current disaffection with the political process. When it comes down to it, the real reason for my silence on class is simply that it does not lend itself to the same kind of solutions. This is as much a failure of political imagination as any more theoretically driven distinction.

II

This point opens up the second area that has been relatively untouched in my discussion so far, which is the very status of representative democracy, and the way it can block more ambitious proposals for extending the incidence and scope of democracy. The preoccupation with sexual or racial exclusions tends to focus attention on the composition of existing élites, whose remarkable homogeneity is what first strikes the excluded observer. Earlier concerns with class-based exclusions usually pushed critics towards a more sceptical indictment of the limits of representative democracy. It seemed all too apparent that a process of democratic representation which centred on electing representatives to national office would continue to disadvantage working-class people, and that a more radical scenario was required to spread the democracy more resolutely around. The places where democracy should be practised then became an even more burning issue than what happened in the conventionally political sphere. In G. D. H. Cole's version of guild socialism, this developed into a functional democracy in which those interests involved in production or distribution would be directly represented in the bodies that carry out the function;[4] in the early work of Carole Pateman or the later work of Robert Dahl, it developed into an argument for workplace democracy;[5] in recent formulations of associative demo-

[4] G. D. H. Cole, *Guild Socialism Re-Stated* (London, 1920).
[5] C. Pateman, *Participation and Democratic Theory* (Cambridge, 1970); R. A. Dahl, *A Preface to Economic Democracy* (Cambridge, 1985).

cracy, it has developed into a case for voluntary and self-governing associations that will take upon themselves many of the responsibilities now claimed by central government.[6]

The arguments for associative democracy are particularly pertinent here, for they are often developed against the background of new social movements, and explicitly acknowledge the way these have altered the roll-call of political actors. Paul Hirst, for example, argues that 'politics is moving away from the great left–right oppositions created in the nineteenth century', and he stresses 'the rise of new political forces that cannot be accommodated on the old political spectrum'.[7] His argument parallels much of what I have said in my case for a new politics around representation: that politics used to be organized around a largely class-derived 'social' question; and that the subsequent differentiation, around issues of gender equality or the prevalence of racism, generates forces that are 'too diverse, too concerned with different issues, to be placed on a single spectrum'.[8] But where I have taken this as requiring a greater plurality at the national level—a more heterogeneous bunch to represent us, and charged with representing us in more dimensions—Hirst takes it as requiring a greater plurality in self-governing voluntary associations. The state remains too much tied to the older binary divides to meet the needs of the heterogeneous citizenry.

In most of the scenarios for associational or associative democracy, the powers and responsibilities of central government would be severely curtailed. Federal and regional governments, for example, would retain the responsibility for raising taxes, but would distribute the public funds among recognized associations which would take on most of the responsibility for delivering services. In Philippe Schmitter's variation, central government would issue vouchers to citizens, redeemable against public funds, which they could then distribute to whichever associations they favoured.[9] These associations

---

[6] E.g. J. Matthews, *The Age of Democracy* (Melbourne, 1989); P. Schmitter, 'The Consolidation of Democracy and Representation of Social Groups', *American Behavioral Scientist*, 35/4, 5 (1992); J. Cohen and J. Rogers, 'Secondary Associations and Democratic Governance', *Politics and Society*, 20/4 (1992); P. Hirst, *Associative Democracy* (Cambridge, 1994).

[7] P. Hirst, *Associative Democracy*, (Cambridge, 1994), 8.   [8] Ibid. 9.

[9] P. C. Schmitter, 'The Irony of Modern Democracy and Efforts to Improve its Practice', *Politics and Society*, 20/4 (1992).

might constitute themselves on an ethnic or religious basis, might indeed be organized as all-women collectives; but they would be bound by certain public conditions, which could determine the basis on which they could refuse membership or their procedures for democratic self-goverment. Paul Hirst stresses that most of the conditions would come into play only when the associations sought public funding; otherwise, associations would be free to form on any basis they chose, subject only to very basic conditions.[10] Philippe Schmitter argues that the basic conditions should remain very minimal, including perhaps just the requirement to be non-profit-making, and to demonstrate some democratic process through which the leaders of the association are selected.[11] In either case, the inclusion of the previously excluded is achieved through maximizing the range and number of associations, rather than dictating the arrangements within each.

Joshua Cohen and Joel Rogers suggest a more interventionist version, arguing that conditions could be set in such a way as to promote deliberative behaviour.[12] Through a combination of taxes, subsidies, and legal sanctions, groups could be fashioned so as to promote the organized representation of presently excluded interests, and encourage the members to be more other-regarding in their aims:[13] those groups that encompass a higher proportion of the relevant population, for example, or address a wider range of issues and concerns, might be favoured over those more narrowly defined.[14] Critics of Cohen and Rogers have noted a tendency to reproduce older configurations by drawing on models from trade union or workplace democracy,[15] but this alone could be treated as an oversight. There is no reason, in principle, why associational democracy

---

[10] Thus: 'the Society for the Propagation of Racial Abuse would be outlawed, associations would be compelled to distribute audited accounts to their members, and to count one person as one vote': Hirst, *Associative Democracy*, 192.

[11] Schmitter, 'Irony of Modern Democracy', 511.

[12] Cohen and Rogers, 'Secondary Associations'.   [13] Ibid. 425.

[14] Ibid. 428–30.

[15] See the contributions by E. M. Inmergut, P. C. Schmitter, and I. M. Young to the special issue on associative democracy in *Politics and Society*, 20/4 (1992). On Schmitter's reading, for example, 'Cohen and Rogers are trying to ensure that class—capital and labour in their most encompassing organisational forms—will continue to occupy a predominant role in the policy process at the expense of more diversified sectional and professional cleavages and against the rising tide of less "productively" defined interests'. Schmitter, 'Irony of Modern Democracy', 510.

cannot extend itself to take in the self-governing lesbian collective that wants to provide informational networks to support young lesbians, or the organization of black mothers that works to improve the educational chances of black children. The more fundamental question is whether exclusions from decision-making are better dealt with by increasing the range of opportunities for different groups of citizens to participate in the policy process, or by guaranteeing their presence in elected assemblies.

The level or size of these assemblies is not particularly significant here, for, while I have focused primarily on developments at the national level, my arguments can apply equally well to national or regional or local assemblies, or to the election of governments for cities or towns. It is not really the relationship between centre and locality that is the issue, but rather the relationship between elected, representative assemblies (whose electoral base may be large or small, but will always include all the adults within the area) and self-selected, functionally specific associations. Both can make some claim to be the more democratic or egalitarian. The first gives each citizen an equal right to vote, but the electoral process then generates a separate caste of political representatives, who take upon themselves the decision-making power. The second is not so inclusive, but it gives direct power to those who implement decisions, rather then ceding this to a distant élite. Both can also claim to be the better site for incorporating group difference: the first through the mechanisms I have advocated for achieving a more proportionate distribution of office between different social groups, the second through encouraging heterogeneity and the self-organization of the previously excluded. But the strategies pull in different directions, for equality of access is assured in the first place through achieving a more balanced or proportionate representation, and in the second place by multiplying the possibilities for self-organization. Conditions attached to the second might also appeal to principles of equal or proportionate presence—outlawing racial or sexual discrimination, for example, or making increased funding conditional on including the relevant constituencies—but the emphasis on *voluntary* associations limits how intrusive such conditions can be.

The importance I have attached to changing the composition of elected assemblies does not set me in conflict with additional moves towards associative democracy, though the importance that others have attached to associative democracy might well lead them to disparage my obsession with political élites. (Changing these might still be a legitimate objective, but more appropriately in a footnote capacity.) The one is, in principle, compatible with the other, for the arguments around political presence do not dictate positions on the role of voluntary associations, any more than they dictate positions on the decentralization of political decision-making or the appropriate relationship between various centres of power. But there is one strong sense in which what I have argued for can be achieved only within the more inclusive context of elected, and representative, assemblies. The introduction of the previously excluded is designed to alter the political agenda, and this implies intervention at that point where people engage with the full range of political alternatives and the full spectrum of policy concerns. Opening up space for new initiatives on service delivery or new approaches to conflicts at work does not deal adequately with this. When difference is incorporated through a *laissez-faire* encouragement that allows all differences to flourish, this does not sufficiently establish the conditions for transformation and change.

If political presence matters, it is because existing structures of power and representation have denied the pertinence of excluded perspectives and concerns, and the re-assessments implied in this cannot be tackled through ceding power to a diversity of relatively autonomous voluntary groups. The hope (if not always the expectation) is that increasing the proportion of our representatives who come from disadvantaged and excluded groups will challenge and subsequently modify the basis on which public policy is defined. This can occur only in contexts which bring the differences together: where representatives who originate from one group are confronted with representatives who originate from another, and where the interaction between them produces something new. The only possible forum for this is that more inclusive assembly which draws together representatives from the citizenry as a whole: an assembly that might be local, regional, or national, but should in principle represent us all.

III

The realist student of politics might note at this point that legislative assemblies are not as powerful as they often like to think, and that transforming their gender or ethnic composition can leave untouched all those non-elected institutions that wield equally impressive powers. In the Nordic debates on gender quotas, it was often suggested that women had been allowed into parliament only when the real power had shifted elsewhere, and that the impressively gendered face of electoral politics masked a more traditional male dominance in the corporate structures of the welfare state.[16] Key decisions were being taken outside of parliament by a plethora of public councils, boards, or committees, whose members were largely nominated by civil servants, thus not even by the parties in power. Since the nominees were drawn from the overwhelmingly male constituency of recognized 'experts', combined with the equally male-dominated representatives of what were seen as the key interest groups, women were grossly under-represented. What was then being gained in the legislative assemblies was being lost in institutions elsewhere.

Recent developments in British politics raise parallel concerns over the explosion of so-called 'quangocracy': the proliferation of quasi-non-governmental organizations which now intervene between electors and the directly elected. Members are appointed to these bodies from what is popularly perceived a list of the 'great and the good',[17] and political patronage combines with the old boys' network to throw up the same names again and again. It goes without saying that the resulting composition is profoundly unrepresentative, and the organizations only very tenuously accountable.

The politics of presence seems self-evidently appropriate to these further institutions of governmental power—and, in one sense, is even easier to argue. Where public boards or committees conceive of themselves as including representatives from major interest groups (as tended to be the case in the Nordic countries), they make themselves immediately vulnerable to complaint if they exclude certain key players. The relevant constituencies are then open to contest, and in Norway in particular this became the basis for very successful initiatives to change the gender composition of the corporate

---

[16] H. Holter, *Patriarchy in a Welfare Society* (Oslo, 1984).

[17] With what one hopes was a hint of self-conscious irony, the Public Appointments Unit of the Civil Service Department used to refer to this *officially* as 'The List of the Great and the Good': see A. Davies, 'Patronage and Quasi-Government: Some Proposals for Reform', in A. Barker, (ed.), *Quangos in Britain* (London, 1982), 172.

structures.[18] If group representation is already part of the rationale, this lends itself even more readily than electoral politics to ensuring a fair balance between social groups.

But more typically, those appointing members to public commissions or regulatory bodies will appeal to notions of professionalism, proven 'track record', and expertise in the relevant areas; and these more deliberately sideline any claims to representative legitimacy. The work of these bodies is then defined in non-political terms (perhaps one should say quasi-non-political), and it becomes harder to inject any urgency into the under-representation of particular groups. If those serving on such bodies make no claims about representing discrete social interests—if they pride themselves, on the contrary, on being above the hurly-burly of political life—there is no such immediate opening for any politics of presence. Representation is not the name of their game; neither 'who' nor 'what' is really at stake.

The questions then revolve around two broader issues: what is the role of these bodies in politics, and what is the status of 'technical expertise'? The first is an increasingly live issue in contemporary debate, for the proliferation of quangos is widely perceived as a way of reducing public accountability for what are still public decisions, and there is considerable pressure for reintroducing some element of representative democracy.[19] Critics in Britain have noted that the membership of these bodies is heavily biased towards supporters of the party in power (i.e. that they are not so much above party politics as they sometimes like to pretend), and this suggests one direction of reform which would be more even-handed between political persuasions. This alone would give priority to ideas over social characteristics—and of itself might confirm the under-representation of minority groups—but at least it reopens the debate about what makes such bodies representative. The arguments about social composition usually refer back to a discourse of representation, and as long as this is ruled out of court, it is hard even to start comparing the relative merits of representation by political opinion and representation by social group. Once degrees of representation are

[18] H. M. Hernes, *Welfare State and Woman Power: Essays in State Feminism* (Oslo, 1987).

[19] W. Hall and S. Weir (eds.), *Ego Trip: Extra-Governmental Organisations in the UK and their Accountability* (Democratic Audit of the UK/Charter 88, 1994).

allowed back into the picture, the politics of presence becomes equally applicable to these other institutions of government.

However, even failing such moves toward greater accountability for this plethora of appointed bodies, we can still query whether appeals to technical expertise mask the dominance of dominant groups. Civil servants, for example, are not normally regarded as representatives, but we are still entitled to ask whether their perceptions of the available options are affected by their own more personal formation. In the Australian experience, opening up the higher echelons of the civil service to women proved to have a significant impact on the content and direction of public policy, introducing a series of feminist initiatives that had not been previously considered.[20] Many of these women were appointed explicitly as feminists (as part of a Labor government commitment to transform the decision-making process), and critics might then see this as an illegitimate politicization of a more properly neutral terrain. But the initiative reflected perceptions that the bureaucracy was not as neutral as it liked to proclaim, and that changing the composition of the civil service was a precondition for broadening the range of policy concerns. Who the bureaucrats are (their gender or ethnicity or race) can have a decisive impact on what they propose as desirable or possible, for, while past experience is no sure indicator of current opinion, it would be distinctly odd if it had no influence. If this is the case within the supposedly neutral regions of a career civil service, it is equally (if not even more) pertinent for those appointed to serve on public bodies. The politics of presence does then lend itself to this further extension, even when representativeness is not explicitly at issue.

The more difficult questions arise over the composition of the judiciary, which is notoriously 'unrepresentative' of women or ethnic minorities. Appointments to the US Supreme Court suggest that an informal quota now operates for women and blacks: that one out of the nine judges should be black; that at least one (currently two) should be female. Representations over the composition of the Canadian Supreme Court have variously suggested some form of quota provision for women, Aboriginal peoples, and Québécois—though the last is formulated in the language of ideas rather than

[20] See the essays in S. Watson, *Playing the State: Australian Feminist Interventions* (London, 1990).

presence, emphasizing familiarity with Quebec's legal code. Meanwhile those campaigning for the introduction of a Bill of Rights in Britain often meet up against the criticism that the rights would be open to interpretation by a non-elected judiciary that is overwhelmingly male and white, and that, failing adequate measures to modify the composition of this judiciary, a Bill of Rights would be no use at all.

All these point towards the politics of presence as applicable to the judiciary as well. But the judiciary is peculiarly inhospitable to notions of social representation, for judges—more than anyone— will see themselves as charged with standing above partial interest. The under-representation of women or ethnic minorities may still be regarded as a problem, but it is hard to see how women judges could regard themselves as 'representing' the interests of women, or ethnic minority judges as 'representing' the interests of ethnic minority groups. Special pleading might be appropriate for the barristers, but is surely the opposite of what the judges should do.

Ronald Dworkin has distinguished between what he calls 'choice-sensitive' and 'choice-insensitive' issues,[21] arguing that, while the former depend on the distribution of preferences within the community (hence a fair balance between different groups), the latter are independent of political choice. The only just decision about whether to finance a new road system, for example, would be one that took into account the different needs and preferences within the community. But the decision about whether to kill convicted murderers or outlaw racial discrimination should not, in his view, be regarded as similarly choice-sensitive: the right decision on such issues does not depend 'in any substantial way on how many people want or approve of capital punishment or think racial discrimination unjust'.[22] The implication, of course, is that certain decisions are legitimated only by the representativeness of those who take them, while others stand independently of this. When this is so, the precise composition of the judiciary may not be such a salient concern.

This conclusion, however, would follow only if we believed in impartiality as that 'view from nowhere',[23] untouched by the expe-

---

[21] R. Dworkin, 'What is Equality? 4: What is Political Equality?' *University of San Francisco Law Review*, 22 (1988).

[22] Ibid. 24.

[23] I. M. Young, *Justice and the Politics of Difference* (Princeton, 1990), 100.

riences from which we have come. If, on the contrary, we see the pursuit of impartiality as depending on gathering the views from everywhere, then securing the diversity of the judiciary becomes as important as securing the diversity of the legislative assembly. In both cases, experience will affect our judgement, and a body that draws overwhelmingly on one set of experiences will be limited in its range of concerns. The difference is that, while members of the legislature *can* legitimately engage in special pleading (can constitute themselves as spokespeople for particular interests even while seeking to reach agreement with the others who are present), members of the judiciary cannot so legitimately regard themselves as 'representing' particular concerns. This is an important distinction (as is the parallel distinction between civil servants and elected politicians), and it makes it harder to argue for strict guarantees along the lines of equal or proportionate presence. But the composition of the judiciary is an additional and significant concern, and particularly so where the judiciary adjudicates constitutional concerns.

IV

The politics of presence does then carry wider implications beyond the more limited terrain which this book occupies. Even on this terrain, however, it speaks to a larger ambition. Part of this relates to the conditions that could make our decision-making assemblies more genuinely deliberative. Existing democracies spread themselves along a continuum between the tight disciplines of party politics, that are most clearly exemplified in Britain, and the kind of 'pork-barrel' behaviour that is more commonly associated with politics in the USA. In the first instance, the elected representatives have relatively little room for manœuvre. They can moan, cajole, and press for new policy directions, but if they consistently vote against the policies decided by their party leadership, they may find themselves forced to leave that party and to contest future elections under a different label. In the second instance, the elected representatives are less easily pushed into line, but their dedicated pursuit of sectional or regional interests is equally unfavourable to serious deliberation or debate. The politics of presence implies something other than either of these; for, while it anticipates the introduction of new kinds of interests and concerns (closer to pork-barrel than tight party disciplines), it also anticipates a process in which these will generate a wider range of policy considerations, modifying others and being modified themselves. If the new representatives have no space to express anything other than existing party policy, their inclusion becomes rather symbolic—which matters, but somewhat less than they hoped. If, on the contrary, the new representatives find themselves locked into sectional pursuit of sectional interest, their impact on the political agenda will be merely a function of their numerical weight. Failing the development of more deliberative conditions, the achievement of more equal or proportionate presence will not transform things as much as I claim, for it begins a process that cannot be completed without some additional change.

The other element in the larger ambition relates to the basis on which representatives can claim to represent 'their' people or group. Once we give up on the guarantees that would come with notions of an essential identity, the only sure basis for such claims would lie in alternative mechanisms of accountability that depend on the self-organization of the relevant group. Most radicals now admit to some doubts over the extent of this. Despite rumours of an explosion in political participation,[24] most of us have revised our expectations downwards towards a cautious recognition that citizen involvement is uneven and rarely sustained. People are far more willing to sign petitions than participate in defining objectives, and even those who have thrown themselves into periods of intensive activity usually retreat into the background when the pressures on their lives become too great. Yet the only convincing basis on which representatives can claim to speak for aspirations not yet written into their party's programme is their relationship to organizations or movements that actively formulate group interests and concerns: this is the only way to ensure that what they say has wider purchase. Changing the composition of elected assemblies only improves the representation of excluded groups in what we might call a statistical sense; failing the development of more sustained conditions for consultation and discussion, it is an enabling condition, and still rather a shot in the dark. It is a better guarantee than we enjoy at present, which is enough to make it a political priority. But the real force of political presence lies in this further development.

[24] R. Topf, 'Electoral Participation and Beyond', in H. D. Klingeman and D. Fuchs (eds.), *Citizens and the State* (Oxford, 1995).

Implicit in most of the arguments for equal or proportionate presence is a larger ambition that sees changing the composition of elected assemblies as part of a project for increasing and enhancing democracy. When the arguments are taken out of this context, they have to rely more heavily on the symbolic importance of achieving more 'representative' assemblies; on the political realism that views representatives drawn from one group as ill-equipped either to recognize or to pursue the concerns of citizens drawn from another; and on the negative argument from justice, which asks by what right certain categories of people have ended up monopolizing representation. This is a powerful enough combination to justify the desired reforms, but does not yet capture the full intent. Put back into context, the argument often reveals a more ambitious programme which would alter the balance between citizens and representatives.

We might think here of the further initiatives that have been so typical of women's activities in politics: the use of the open forum, for example, as a way of consulting women in a local community; the report back to women's sections or women's conferences; the presumption of chains of connection that ought to link women politicians to activists from the women's movement. When the Icelandic Women's Party (Kwenna Frambothid) made its first substantial gains on city councils in the course of the 1980s, its newly elected councillors tried to sustain their relationship with the women who had campaigned for their election by setting up weekly meetings in which they could report back on issues arising in the council, and seek advice and feedback on what they ought to do.[25] Over much the same period, a number of local councils in Britain set up women's committees to address the specific needs of women within their area, and these made extensive use of co-option and the open forum as a way of consulting women outside the political parties.[26] Even among those most committed to party politics (and many deliberately stayed outside, in the more amorphous politics of women's

[25] L. Dominelli and G. Jonsdottir, 'Feminist Political Organization in Iceland: Some Reflections on the Experience of Kwenna Frambothid', *Feminist Review*, 36 (1988).

[26] See e.g. S. Goss, 'Women's Initiatives in Local Government', in M. Boddy and C. Fudge (eds.), *Local Socialism? Labour Councils and New Left Alternatives* (London, 1984); J. Edwards, 'Local Government Women's Committees', *Critical Social Policy*, 24 (1988/9); A. Coote and P. Patullo, *Power and Prejudice: Women and Politics* (London, 1990).

movement groups and campaigns), the political party has been viewed as an inadequate vehicle for representation, and women politicians have pursued what they saw as complementary ways of empowering women to make their needs better known. Neither of the examples I have given was a brilliant success: in the first case, the weekly meetings dwindled into fortnightly gatherings of six or so 'tired and disillusioned women';[27] and in both cases, those who came to the meetings or open forums tended to be untypical of women in the area as a whole. However, even if they do not provide exemplars for future representatives to follow, they do testify to the larger ambitions that have surrounded the election of more women.

The case for political presence is best understood in this broader context, and to this extent it confirms Hanna Pitkin's intuition. The argument for a more equitable representation of the two sexes or a more even-handed distribution between different ethnic groups does move in close parallel with arguments for a more participatory democracy. Those concerned with the under-representation of particular social groups look to the development of more deliberatory processes of decision-making within the representative assemblies. They also look to the development of new mechanisms of consultation, perhaps even accountability, that will link representatives more responsively to the various groups' emerging concerns. We do not need this additional ammunition to make the case for immediate reform, but, as a more profound set of issues about democracy and representation, the politics of presence is at its strongest when it is associated with the larger dream.

Easier said than done, and I admit to considerable uncertainty as to what would bring either of these changes about. Recent explorations of deliberative democracy seem more concerned with what is desirable than with what is possible, while appeals to a more active and engaged citizenry often fall on deaf ears. But the factor common to both is their reformulation of the role currently claimed by political parties, and this links them to developments already occurring in the political world. Through much of the nineteenth and twentieth centuries, political parties defined themselves along a spectrum that derived ultimately from divisions by class. The declining salience of this spectrum has already loosened up the character of political par-

---

[27] Dominelli and Jonsdottir, 'Feminist Political Organization in Iceland', 52.

ties, fostering a search for new kinds of party identity and new ways of formulating political divides. The growth of significant third parties in countries (like Britain) which are more used to an alternation between two parties in power is one indication of this.[28] The much discussed 'post-materialist' analysis, which charts the growth of single-issue politics and the impossibility of tracking these along any single left–right divide, is another.[29] Class can no longer operate as the master key which unlocks the major policy alternatives, and there is no obvious new candidate that can fill the vacated space.

In this diverse and diffuse context, it is harder to wrap up the citizens into neat packages of competing ideas. Political parties become more overtly what they have always in reality been: coalitions of different groups and objectives and interests, whose concerns have to be brought out into the open and more vigorously and continuously discussed. It can no longer be presumed that all policy alternatives are already known or already in play, and political parties then have to reach out to previously excluded constituencies and enable them to redefine the political agenda. Nor can it be presumed that all legitimate concerns will fit together in easy combination. Political parties then have to moderate some of their tighter disciplines, accept a greater degree of autonomy for the elected representatives, and recognize the validity of continuous discussion and debate.

Whether this will actually happen is harder to say. Perhaps the class issues that gave twentieth-century politics its urgency and bite will simply fall off the agenda, to be replaced by a bland sameness between parties that reduces both representation and choice. Perhaps there will be even further capitulation to the experts, or more passive fatalism among the citizens. What we can say, however, is that these outcomes are far less likely to emerge with the development of a politics of presence. Politics does not lend itself readily to guarantees, but this is one pretty safe prediction.

---

[28] The character of the British electoral system (single-member constituencies, electing whoever gets a simple majority) means that the two-party system will continue to dominate at national level, but local councils are now far more variegated, and many are governed by party coalitions, where no one party holds majority power.

[29] See e.g. the essays in R. Dalton and M. Kuchler (eds.), *Challenging the Political Order: New Social and Political Movements in Western Democracies* (Cambridge, 1990).

BIBLIOGRAPHY

Abrams, K., ' "Raising Politics Up": Minority Political Participation and Section 2 of the Voting Rights Act', *New York University Law Review*, 63/3 (1988).

—— 'Relationships of Representation in Voting Rights Act Jurisprudence', *Texas Law Review*, 71/7 (1993).

Abramson, J., 'The Jury and Democratic Theory', *Journal of Political Philosophy*, 1/1 (1993).

Arblaster, A., *Democracy* (Milton Keynes, 1987).

Axworthy, T. S., and Trudeau, P. E. (eds.), *Towards a Just Society: The Trudeau Years* (Ontario, 1990).

Bacchi, C., *Same Difference: Feminism and Sexual Difference* (London, 1990).

Barber, B., *Strong Democracy* (Berkeley, 1984).

Barrett, M., and Phillips, A. (eds.), *Destabilizing Theory: Contemporary Feminist Debates* (Cambridge, 1993).

Barry, B., 'Political Accommodation and Consociational Democracy', *British Journal of Political Science*, 5/4 (1975).

—— 'Is Democracy Special?', in P. Laslett and J. Fishkin (eds.), *Philosophy, Politics and Society* (Oxford, 1979).

Bashevkin, S. (ed.), *Women and Politics in Western Europe* (London, 1985).

Bayefsky, A. F., 'The Effect of Aboriginal Self-Government on the Rights and Freedoms of Women', *Network Analyses: Reactions*, (October 1992).

Beetham, D., *Auditing Democracy in Britain*. The Democratic Audit of the United Kingdom, Paper I (Charter 88 Trust) (London, 1993).

Beitz, C. R., *Political Equality: An Essay in Democratic Theory* (Princeton, 1989).

Bock, G., and James, S. (eds.), *Beyond Equality and Difference* (London, 1993).

Browning, R. P., Marshall, D. R., and Tabb, D. H., *Protest Is Not Enough: The Struggle of Blacks and Hispanics for Equality in Urban Politics* (Berkeley, 1984).

—— —— —— (eds.), *Racial Politics in American Cities* (New York, 1990).

Burnheim, J., *Is Democracy Possible?* (Cambridge, 1985).

Cairns, A. C., *Disruptions: Constitutional Struggles from the Charter to Meech Lake* (Toronto, 1991).

C. Fudge (eds.), *Local Socialism? Labour Councils and New Left Alternatives* (London, 1984).

Gottlieb, R. (ed.), *Tradition, Counter-Tradition, Politics: Dimensions of Radical Philosophy* (Philadephia, 1994).

Green, P., *The Pursuit of Inequality* (New York, 1981).

Grofman, B., 'Should Representatives be Typical of their Constituents?' in B. Grofman, A. Lijphart, R. B. McKay, and H. A. Scarrow (eds.), *Representation and Redistricting Issues* (Lexington, Mass., 1982).

—— and Davidson, C., 'Postcript: What Is the Best Route to a Color-Blind Society?' in B. Grofman and C. Davidson (eds.), *Controversies in Minority Voting* (Washington, DC, 1992).

—— —— (eds.), *Controversies in Minority Voting: The Voting Rights Act in Perspective* (Washington DC, 1992).

—— and Handley, L., 'The Impact of the Voting Rights Act on Black Representation in Southern State Legislatures', *Legislative Studies Quarterly*, 16/1 (1991).

—— Lijphart, A., McKay, R. B., and Scarrow, H. A. (eds.), *Representation and Redistricting Issues* (Lexington, Mass, 1982).

Guinier, L., 'Keeping the Faith: Black Voters in the Post-Reagan Era', *Harvard Civil Rights–Civil Liberties Law Review*, 24 (1989); reprinted in L. Guinier, *The Tyranny of the Majority* (New York, 1994).

—— 'No Two Seats: The Elusive Quest for Political Equality', *Virginia Law Review*, 77/8 (1991); reprinted in L. Guinier, *The Tyranny of the Majority* (New York, 1994).

—— 'The Triumph of Tokenism: The Voting Rights Act and the Theory of Black Success', *Michigan Law Review*, 89/5 (1991); reprinted in L. Guinier, *The Tyranny of the Majority* (New York, 1994).

—— 'Voting Rights and Democratic Theory: Where Do We Go From Here?' in B. Grofman and C. Davidson (eds.), *Controversies in Minority Voting* (Washington, DC, 1992).

—— 'Groups, Representation, and Race-Conscious Districting: A Case of the Emperor's Clothes', *Texas Law Review*, 71/7 (1993); reprinted in L. Guinier, *The Tyranny of the Majority* (New York, 1994).

—— *The Tyranny of the Majority: Fundamental Fairness in Representative Democracy* (New York, 1994).

Gunew, S., and Yeatman, A. (eds.), *Feminism and the Politics of Difference* (Sydney, 1993).

Gutmann, A. (ed.), *Multiculturalism and the 'Politics of Recognition'*, (Princeton, 1992).

Habermas, J., 'Struggles for Recognition in Constitutional States', *European Journal of Philosophy*, 1/2 (1993).

Hall, W., and Weir, S. (eds.), *Ego Trip: Extra-Governmental Organisations in the UK and their Accountability* (Democratic Audit of the UK/Charter 88, 1994).

Hare, T., *Treatise on the Election of Representatives* (London, 1859).

Hamlin, A. and Pettit, P. (eds.), *The Good Polity: Normative Analysis of the State* (Oxford, 1989).

Held, V., 'Mothering versus Contract', in J. J. Mansbridge (ed.), *Beyond Self-Interest* (Chicago, 1990).

Hernes, H. M., *Welfare State and Woman Power: Essay in State Feminism* (Oslo, 1987).

Hirst, P., *Associative Democracy* (Cambridge, 1994).

Holter, H., *Patriarchy in a Welfare Society* (Oslo, 1984).

Issacharoff, S., 'Polarized Voting and the Political Process: The Transformation of Voting Rights Jurisprudence', *Michigan Law Review*, 90/7 (1992).

Jacquette, J., 'Power as Ideology: A Feminist Analysis', in J. S. Stiehm (ed.), *Women's Views of the Political World of Men* (New York, 1985).

Jonasdottir, A., 'On the Concept of Interest, Women's Interests, and the Limitation of Interest Theory', in K. B. Jones and A. Jonasdottir, *The Political Interests of Women* (London, 1988).

Jones, K. B., *Compassionate Authority: Democracy and the Representation of Women* (New York, 1993).

—— and Jonasdottir, A., *The Political Interests of Women* (London, 1988).

Kateb, G., 'The Moral Distinctiveness of Representative Democracy', *Ethics*, 91/3 (1981).

Kome, P., *The Taking of Twenty-Eight: Women Challenge the Constitution* (Toronto, 1983).

Kukathas, C., 'Are There Any Cultural Rights?', *Political Theory*, 20/1 (1992).

—— 'Cultural Rights Again: A Rejoinder to Kymlicka', *Political Theory*, 20/4 (1992).

Kymlicka, W., *Liberalism, Community, and Culture* (Oxford, 1989).

—— 'The Rights of Minority Cultures: Reply to Kukathas', *Political Theory*, 20/1 (1992).

—— 'Group Representation in Canadian Politics', in F. L. Seidle (ed.), *Equity and Community: The Charter, Interest Advocacy and Representation* (Montreal, 1993).

—— 'Three Forms of Group-Differentiated Citizenship in Canada', paper presented at the conference on Democracy and Difference, Yale University, 1993.

—— *Multicultural Citizenship: A Liberal Theory of Minority Rights* (Oxford, 1995).

:h, S., and Studlar, D. T., 'Multi-Member Districts and the
presentation of Women: Evidence from Britain and the United States',
nal of Politics, 52/2 (1990).

, W. J., *The Truly Disadvantaged: The Inner City, the Underclass,*
ublic Policy (Chicago, 1987).

, A., 'Voice and Representation in the Politics of Difference', in
w and A. Yeatman (eds.), *Feminism and the Politics of Difference*
, 1993).

R., *Justice and the Politics of Difference* (Princeton, 1990).

Scan and Communicative Democracy', in R. Gottlieb (ed.),
Counter-Tradition, Politics: Dimensions of Radical Philosophy
a, 1994).

P e's
Skje and
(1 the

Eli ', in
Smith ative
Rig
(199 ty', in
Special ondon,
Stasiuli
Femi nocracy
A. Y
1993). Nation
Stiehm, J
1984). Pitkin's
Still, J., 'P ics', Acta
Sunstein,
(1988). ist Studies,
—— 'Prefe
—— 'Neut roup-Based
Pornogra mbia Law
(1992).
—— 'Demo
J. E. Roem ons (London,
Tate, K., Fro
Elections (N New Canada
Taylor, C., 'Sh
(eds.), Optio don, 1994).
—— 'The Polit resentation
and the 'Polit

INDEX